BRAND YOU ECONOMICS

TIMELESS, TANGIBLE PRINCIPLES & TOOLS TO BUILD YOUR BRAND LEGACY

ARNT ERIKSEN

authorHOU

D1719617

AuthorHouse™ UK
1663 Liberty Drive
Bloomington, IN 47403 USA
www.authorhouse.co.uk
Phone: UK TFN: 0800 0148641 (Toll Free inside the UK)
*   UK Local: 02036 956322 (+44 20 3695 6322 from outside the UK)*

Published by AuthorHouse 05/27/2021

ISBN: 978-1-6655-8437-1 (sc)
ISBN: 978-1-6655-8436-4 (hc)
ISBN: 978-1-6655-8435-7 (e)

Print information available on the last page.

This book is printed on acid-free paper.

CONTENTS

To my parents, Tove and Kåre, who supported me, guided me, and gave me everything I needed to become the person I am today.

And to my amazing kids, Arnt David, Kris Isak, and Natalie, for keeping me accountable, motivated, and proud; unconditional love for always.

It's kind of fun to do
the impossible.

—Walt Disney

FOREWORD

I used to hate speaking in front of people. I got so nervous, dry mouth, racing heart, trembling voice, just hopeless, but then, in 2008, that changed. First I spoke in front of forty colleagues about the trends I learned about from an event I attended, and since then, I have been speaking on stages all over the world: the Nordics (of course), the United Kingdom, the Netherlands, the USA, Canada, Australia, Iceland, and audiences ranging from twenty (the worst) to three thousand (easy). I still get nervous, but in a good way. Now I thrive and love being on stage to share what I know. I made (what I thought) the impossible, possible, and I love it. I usually start my keynotes and public speaking presentations with a picture of the tiny island where I first grew up. It is a small, rigid island in the cluster of islands known as Lofoten, situated in the north of Norway.

There, in this bridge-connected group of islands, is an island by the name of Hadsel Island, with a small village named Stokmarknes, a small town with approximately eighteen hundred inhabitants. At the age of four, I had my first memories of significance, and my network consisted of my mother, father, my elder brother, Ken-Tore, and my closest friends: Steinar, Claus, Julie, and Elisabeth.

Before my family came to Stokmarknes, we had moved around in the country quite a lot, as my brother was struggling with asthma in his early years (he is four years older than me). First it was Mosjøen, the city where I was born, but we only stayed for six months, then came Harstad, Fagernes, Røros, and Tromsø before we ended up living in Stokmarknes in 1975. I often get asked by people, when told of all the places I lived in my early years, whether my father was in the army, as they tend to move quite a bit when they are excelling in level and grade, but nothing could be further from the truth, though it might seem as the most natural and obvious explanation. I do have a lot of army people in my family, but not my dad.

My dad is a printer, and in Stokmarknes, both my parents worked at the region's book-printing shop. My dad had a C-level manager job, and my mom worked as a typist on what would be considered the first computers of the time within the industry.

I always came by their workplace after school and watched the huge machinery produce wonderful books and impressive brochures and magazines. I loved to play with the old wood-framed letters with sans and serif fonts in every conceivable size, and I used to combine the letters and write my name and other sentences, which I then pressed onto beautiful structured paper with various colours. I also came across the printshop's stack of 24k gold leaf sheets, used to create the imprinted titles onto the cover of books. I'm pretty sure I cost them a small fortune, as I loved to create different designs and illustrations with the sheets of gold.

I guess this is the point in time when my interest for graphic design and visual storytelling came to life. This is where I had my first encounter with the process of creating a book from cover to cover, seeing the finished product, using the various techniques and machines to make the different elements that ended up in this beautiful book, with the amazing smell of quality paper with elegant gold letters on the front of the cover. It was craftsmanship at its best of my knowledge back then, and I was fascinated and impressed by how it all came to life.

My dad was a very hard-working man, no stranger to the midnight oil, and he worked with passion and an emerging drive to deliver the highest standard of quality; he pushed himself and his staff to their best, which sometimes included working over the weekend to meet a deadline and deliver as promised. I can easily connect my own moral of hard work and standards directly linked to seeing my dad work as much and hard as he did.

After five years at this small place in Lofoten (look it up, and you'll be impressed with the nature), it was time to leave the north of Norway and head on south, to a slightly bigger and more picturesque town called Grimstad, a small place with deeply religious inhabitants.

It is hard to explain the contrast from the move of almost two thousand kilometres to the south of Norway, where everything was softer, warmer, stranger, but yet more pleasant. The majestic mountains from the north were replaced with softer and flatter countryside and coastline. My parents sold us the idea of the warmer summers, and when it rained, it was hard, intense, but short, which was very welcomed. They convinced us, and the small town of 14,800 was a new and exciting step on our journey.

My father's first job was at the local newspaper, where he stayed for a year. He then took the step from being a worker to becoming an entrepreneur. In 1983, he started his own printshop with a friend he had worked with at the newspaper. My mother joined them some months later to help with typing and administrative tasks.

As a kid, it was priceless to be able to be a part of my parents' start-up, building a sustainable business from scratch, getting their first small group of clients, establishing a credible reputation. I spent every single moment of my free time at the printshop. It was natural, as they both had to work hard in the beginning to build the business and make ends meet. I remember helping them with all the finishing work: gluing, assembling, stapling, and packaging the finished products for delivery. My brother and I spent the weekends assembling and stapling the program for the local soccer team before their home games. It was a valuable lesson to be part of assisting your parents in creating their own dream.

After some years, I moved up the ranks and was given access to the heavy machinery: the Heidelberg press. I printed everything from business cards, letterheads, and stationery up to the full four-colour brochures, all that at the age of thirteen. I felt both proud and accomplished.

More importantly, I learned many critical things during that period of time in my life: To make things happen, you have to work hard; the beauty of process; the importance of taking responsibility, delivering high-quality service to our clients, and building strong relationships and loyal customers were all key. At my parents' printshop, I was introduced to the four-colour process (CMYK), explored the vast and amazing world of typography and letterheads, and developed a strong passion for craftsmanship. Combined with high-quality standards, we had a killer combination.

This was also where I experienced the study of economics for the first time, with being hands-on with production, distribution, and consumption of printed goods. I understood the process of the business, how the clients entered the store with an order, or a need, and then seeing how the product was made from A-Z in the shop, delivered to the client, only to later see it circulated in the community. It made a strong impression on me.

Another thing I learned at the printshop was that I didn't want to be a printer. This was, of course, a huge disappointment to my dad, as he was expecting and hoping I would take over the family business one day. I was more keen and driven to create the ideas, layouts, and designs being printed and produced, than the printing job itself.

So at the age of sixteen, it was time for me to move out and begin my journey, start my designated walk of life. I went to another small town, which had one of the country's two universities for the craft of visual communication.

This was the next important step on my path to where I am now, and I hope you'll bear with me. The reason I want to share this with you in this book is so that you understand the context of where I am coming from, my learnings and collected experience I have acquired over the past thirty-odd years.

Brand has always been important to me and something I have been passionate about since back in school, when I designed logos, product names, packaging, and hand-made typography. I also found my love for advertising, getting familiar with the masters: Ogilvy, Bates, Leo Burnett, and Bill Burnbach.

What I am proud of and what has shaped me over the years is the fact that I have persistence, stamina, and the gusto to make shit happen. I never give up, and if one way doesn't work, I try another. This has given me opportunities to both succeed and fail. I've owned my own agency, I've had companies went bankrupt and failed miserably, but I've also worked with and for some amazing agencies: Recommended, Isobar, Creuna, DDB, and Ogilvy, and I think the fact that I've failed a few times as an entrepreneur has given me the strength, insights, understanding, and empathy of what it means to have your own company, to burn the midnight oil, to believe in what you set out to do, to be crazy enough to think that you are going to change the world.

I've learned a lot of valuable lessons over the course of my life. Some, granted, I would have preferred avoiding at that particular moment in time: having to fire a colleague, or to inform the staff their paycheque will be delayed, or the worst message, to say that I've failed as a leader and the company has gone out of business.

Hard-earned lessons, but they made me who I am, and I am stronger, I am wiser, and I also understand and respect the life and path of an entrepreneur. What I lack in business skills may be compensated for by understanding the importance of brand and my marketing skills. I have worked on and with some amazing brands over the past decades, from small local businesses with amazing potential and owners, to national, regional, and global brands. We faced different challenges, but I've discovered some common drivers and barriers that can be solved by focusing on the right principles, then developing methods and assets to solve any problem the brand is facing.

This is the process I love. This is why I love what I do. This is why I love being a mentor and advisor to companies, and also why I decided to write this first book of mine, to share some of my knowledge, insight, and passion with you.

I am going to give you some key learnings and share my experience with you on how I went from being a kid from a small Norwegian island to a global citizen in this world of ours with its more than 7 billion people, all done with the insight, ambition, touchpoints, and blueprint I am going to share with you, simply put, my marketing principles and methodology.

I have come to the point where I'm more or less 3 degrees of separation from anyone I'd like to connect with in this world. All this because I followed certain principles, created some of my own, and utilized them throughout my career.

As for marketing, that passion came at a later stage, because I didn't fully grasp the concept that advertising is just one of many aspects of marketing. But when I realized it is the study and management of exchange relationships, the actual business process of identifying, anticipating, and satisfying customers' needs, wants, and desires, that's when it hit me. It's about understanding human behaviour, interactions, and perceptions in conjunction with a brand. Fascinating.

My ambition for writing this book is to share these insights and principles, which I hope can become useful, tangible tools in your everyday business life and assist you in building your legacy, your brand, that can outlast this lifetime and the next.

Welcome to *Brand You Economics*, timeless, tangible tools and principles to ensure your brand's legacy.

Men of principle are always bold, but those who are bold are not always men of principle.

—Confucius

CHAPTER 1

INCEPTION

After graduating art school with a three-year degree in visual communication, I entered the world of advertising. In retrospect, I think I entered it at the perfect time, although at that point, I did not feel that way, but hold that thought.

Back in 1991, the advertising industry was at its peak in Norway. The agencies at the time were swimming in money. This was back in the days when art directors and copywriters made TV Commercials (TVCs) for their clients—and planning and execution required the whole team of creatives, producers, film crew, and actors to shoot commercials in some remote location, preferably where the weather was more pleasant, warmer, and more convenient, especially if the season was winter, which often happened to be the case.

Alas, this was the start of the downfall of many traditional agencies, as displeased customers became tired of pouring massive amounts of their money into the agency pockets without receiving results and proof of where the money was spent and if it actually generated results at all.

At the agency I was working for at the time as junior art director, the same thing happened. My first experience only a few weeks into the job was presented in a conversation between one of the key account managers and the managing director. One of our clients had asked for a full-spread ad in a magazine, but the manager was tired of the client. He instructed the KAM to double the budget for the job. If the client objected, well, good riddance, but if they accepted, well, at least they got well compensated for having this shitty client.

I was completely surprised and shocked by this way of treating a client. There were several similar instances, and needless to say, it had to come to an end. As I was the last one to be hired, I was the first one to be fired when the company cut personnel. Recession in the advertising industry was a fact, and the ad-men El Dorado was ending. The credibility of the agencies was at its lowest of all time.

I decided to head south and got hired as art director at one of the best agencies in the region at the time, where I stayed for about two challenging yet rewarding years. Then in 1996, I followed in my father's footsteps and became an entrepreneur. I founded my first advertising agency and became a strong competitor to the other established agencies within the first year. After several years of running my own shop, I came to the conclusion that this was too much for my creative spirit, so I joined forces with my fiercest competitors.

Together, we grew to be the largest agency in the region, and we later expanded to the Nordics, with offices in Norway, Denmark, Sweden, and Finland. At that point, I had obtained valuable knowledge and vast experience since I had practised almost every position possible in an agency: consultant; secretary; project manager; planner; strategist; advisor; art director; copywriter; creative director; and CEO. I'd done them all and was completely familiar with the process of the clients, from brief to idea, to visuals, to finished advertisement. I was doing what I set out to do at the age of sixteen. I was an adman (madman), doing what I was passionate about, with a drive as an art director and advisor for my selection of great brands, having a decade producing solid and creative work for my clients.

Then in 2009, the recession kicked in all across the world. Norway didn't get any direct impact, per se, but some of our regional and national clients that traded with Europe reduced our earnings quite drastically.

This, combined with a restructuring process led by poor management, made me realize I was on a ship about to get into rough seas and take in a lot of water and possibly go down. I needed to act quickly and make some drastic and life-changing decisions. I needed to rethink my life and perspectives.

Now, hold that thought.

The New World

> We have always found that, if our principles were right,
> the area over which they were applied did not matter.
> Size is only a matter of the multiplication table.
>
> —Henry Ford

Let me put things a bit more in context. In 2007, I was still holding the position as art director, in tandem with a close colleague of mine, who was my copywriter. One day, I was summoned to the office of our CEO. Being quite curious and hungry for knowledge, I was one of the few people at the agency who embraced the wonderful new world of the Internet, beyond news sites and corporate pages. I was told—not asked—to be the bridge between the advertising department and the interactive department, with the new title of interactive creative director (iCD). I must admit I was somewhat inspired by Steve Jobs and Apple and found a little bit of joy in adding a small "i" in front of the creative title. The reason for this new position was the fact that I had the most knowledge about social media in the agency and believed them to be the future. I guess it's safe to say they and I were both right.

At the same time, it was necessary to integrate the traditional advertising and interactive department with a wider offering to our clients. It was the dawn of social media, which at the time consisted of Facebook, Twitter, Friendfeed, and a few other networks and tools. I went all in and spent from fifteen to eighteen hours a day listening, learning, talking, engaging, and creating a presence online. I started following the advice of Guy Kawasaki, whom I had great respect and admiration for from way back when he was the Apple evangelist (an awesome title).

To my great joy, he had fully embraced the world of social media and was evangelizing the potential of engagement through these new channels.

I didn't know it at the time, and I was quite reluctant in the beginning, but it turned out to be a complete turn of events in my professional career and personal life. At this point in time, I spent every moment involved in this new world and learning from the thought leaders at the time. I sent more than 250 tweets a day and created content for my blogs on a weekly basis.

Let's return to 2009 and the start of the end of my stay in the south of Norway, as the agency was starting to crack and break apart. I was already established as a thought leader in the Norwegian community, writing content in both Norwegian and English. I did a video podcast with a friend of mine in true Diggnation style (google it). I used Facebook actively, but my most engaging platform was Twitter, where I spent hours upon hours each day engaging with local and international friends from all over the world. So in June 2009, I reached out on Twitter to some of my strongest connections and influencers in Norway, and an hour later, I had more than a dozen job offers. A week later, I signed a contract with *the* social media consultancy agency at the time, where I joined the team as a senior advisor and creative director.

In the transition from the old job to the new, I took a couple of trips to New York, where I met some amazing people, people I had connected with online and had come to be inspired by. I truly fell in love with the city and can safely say that this moment in time turned out to be a tipping point in my life.

Even though the way things happened in my life might appear quite random, I can in retrospect see the clear path and series of events happening based on the fact that I focused on how I could position myself and build a brand around my persona, leveraging the skills and knowledge I had obtained over the years.

So are you ready to get all the principles, tools, insight, and knowledge I have accumulated over the past decades? (Well, not all of it, but what is relevant to this book. Yes, there might be more books coming.)

Okay. As Churchill said, "Onwards and upwards."

Introduction

As to methods there may be a million and then some, but principles are few. The man who grasps principles can successfully select his own methods. The man who tries methods, ignoring principles, is sure to have trouble.

The above quote is attributed to efficiency expert Harrington Emerson, who popularized the concept of scientific management, which analysed and synthesized workflow. Though he died in the early 1930s, many of his principles are still in use and taught in business classes today. Emerson's theory of efficiency and principled thinking focuses largely on the idea that if one wants to master the fine, intricate details that make up the world of business (be it traditional print marketing or new, digital marketing that focuses on engaging users online), one need to have a firm grasp of the basic qualities that separate a consumer within the target market of one channel from the consumers of a different company, media outlet, or product.

5

Principles

> Principles don't change, people do.
>
> —Carlos Wallace

Looking back, I do believe that my background in the basics of printing and my later experience in advertising paved the way for my success in social media and the possibilities that have become realities in my pursuit to assist brands in connecting with their audiences.

I understood the principles of communication and marketing, and soon realized that I had an advantage beyond other consultants focusing on digital and social media. These tools are not a substitute for traditional advertising, but an addition to the marketing mix. Most of the speciality agencies that emerged as social media agencies were solely skilled on the platforms with newly educated PR or communication staff. Very few, if any, had taken the holistic approach from a marketing perspective to the new media landscape, connecting the essential dots between paid, owned, and earned media.

Cross channel marketing was something we early adopters were starting to define, but not something that the established global agencies spoke of (or even practised in an effective way). I felt quite confident that this was my time, which later was confirmed by both my colleagues and clients. All my experience, my curiosity, my hunger for understanding and utilizing this new toolbox became the foundation of this book and the principles of *Brand You Economics*.

Before we dig into these principles, we must look at the media landscape and the potential that lies in the connections that can turn any stranger into a customer, and then make them our friend, and then turn them into a brand advocate.

At no time in history has the concept of returning to the principles of marketing and target market research been more relevant than today, when society offers endless interconnectivity. While there are a vast number of effective marketing methods that can reach your customers in the online sphere, there is a growing trend among brands and marketers alike to produce as much content as possible, spread across a multitude of platforms. An attitude valuing quantity over quality has gripped the world of digital marketing by its throat, as brands continue to churn out as much content as humanly possible, with little strategy. Marketing principles have effectively been thrown out the window, as even the most seasoned of experts figures out how to navigate this new world of online content creation by throwing an endless amount of jumbled ideas into production and seeing what sticks. The end result is often very little.

This phenomenon, which we will dub content pollution, is perhaps a natural result of the massive amount of noise now being created online, thanks to the spread of social media. In previous years, advertisers could count on there being relatively little competition for consumer's attention, thanks to the high cost of entry. After all, the mom-and-pop grocery store would never have enough money in the 1970s to run a TV commercial alongside the latest ad for Coca-Cola. Today, all one needs to become an online influencer and to command the attention of an entire sphere of potential customers is a smartphone with a camera.

Naturally, this has led to a huge influx of content; coupled with the rise of social media, nearly everyone you meet is an influencer or content creator in some way, even if the only thing they are creating is a rogue Facebook status or TikTok video. This new culture of noise has thrown marketers into a frenzy; many of them are equally unfamiliar with this new world of constant connection. They see themselves as competing with everyone, from other brands' social media teams to the everyday man posting on Twitter for the amusement of his friends, the temptation is strong to produce as much content as possible; how else can one effectively fight back against this endless stream of noise being put into the digital world?

The key lies in returning to our principles as marketers: the principles of targeted advertising, knowing your customer base, and understanding the different users and their behaviours in each individual content consumption outlet. There's no need for your brand to contribute to the clutter and waste money with incongruent marketing. As a marketer, take the time to refresh yourself on who your valuable customer is, and read up on the differences between social media outlets and channels. One or two well-thought-out activations will always be endlessly more effective than posting generic content to every platform. After all, there are a million methods and then some, but you, as the expert in your customer base, are the only one who can determine which will be most effective for you.

World of Media

> The journey is the reward.
>
> —Steve Jobs

In this age of narcissism, where all these tools are being used to boost our own egos and to promote ourselves and our conceivable strengths, we all tell the story we want the world to think of us. We try to control how we are being perceived by our family, close friends, acquaintances, and coworkers. The good thing is that everyone now has the chance to reach out to their audience and build their brand by focusing on their strengths and skills.

Average people just want to portray their best life using Instagram, Facebook, Twitter, or the next popular platform to share updates focusing on the everyday events in life. But why? What is this need to spend time and efforts to take that perfect #selfie or the dish of the evening, or simply sharing all the cool stuff you are surrounded by? Why are there X amount of Converse pictures on Instagram? Why is it that food, feet, and pets are the most published motifs on social networks?

What does it mean? How real is the story being told? Are we reducing the credibility of the networks? Our activity makes them lose their value and become less authentic. As we produce more content than ever before, we are also more immune to all the impressions that we are bombarded with each and every day. I remember back in 2009, when I had my first keynote presentation, I quoted a report from Forrester that claimed people experienced more than three thousand impressions in a day, which is equivalent to what someone had in a lifetime fifty years ago.

Four years later, the number of impressions, according to Forrester, was more than ten thousand. We are expected to deal with more than three times as many impressions now, in one day.

This is a massive challenge. How can we as brands ever manage to reach our audience when there is so much noise? And it is not only noise from us and all of our competitors. Now we are competing with our own audience, as they are producing massive amounts of content as well, which in all truthfulness is both a blessing and a curse.

For one thing, people don't like to be too involved in other people's lives when it comes to issues and problems. We can be supportive, but we'd rather just see the positive and glamorous side from our friends and family. It's a fine line, and very few manage to balance it perfectly, which is okay. After all, we are only human, and perfection is the enemy of the great.

When building a brand, you need to be aware of where you are going to connect with your audience, whether you are building your personal brand or a corporate brand.

It's important to do thorough research and figure out where, how, and when to connect and engage with your target group and, most importantly, define why they should care.

On the organizational level, it is necessary to base your communication and media mix on the brand vision, mission culture, and values. It is imperative to build a strategy that is known and integrated (read: understood) with everyone in the company and to create tactics based upon the strategy on an operational level within the organization. Everyone needs to be familiar with the strategy and tactics, for one obvious reason. Now more than ever, you and your colleagues are internal brand ambassadors with connections that reach far beyond the tribe of the company and their family and friends.

Ric Dragon, cofounder and former CEO of Dragon Search, describes this in his 2012 book, *Social Marketology*. He talks about the importance of developing an internal brand ambassador program:

> An internal brand ambassador program can be a way of including employees throughout the organization of your social media efforts. This group of people can include your blog writers and Twitter, Facebook, LinkedIn and other social media platform participants. Provide them with training and even a training guide covering the organization's social media policies and voice.
>
> If you're looking to integrate the whole organization into social media, start with marketing and then set up a brand ambassador (BA) program for the other employees.
>
> How a program like this gets rolled out to employees will vary by organization. Participation may be voluntary or assigned through departments. Some organizations

don't allow employees to engage in social media on behalf of the organization unless they've been through training.

Consider rolling out a BA program in phases and start small. For instance, 12 participants each blogging once a quarter would provide a new blogpost weekly.

Think through the goals of the program. For example, is the goal to foster internal thought leadership or is it to increase external interactions with customers?

As you can imagine I tend to focus my attention from day one, to having a strategy and tactics in place as soon as possible, as well as some clearly defined principles that are related to the company and its employees. This will make it easier to build a strong brand that engages and attracts an audience beyond your company's four walls.

Dragon goes further and talks about the importance of developing a customer brand ambassador program. The approach to a customer BA program will depend on your brand and the target ambassadors. If your brand has an audience that's highly engaged and passionately involved, it is easy to get them involved without any form of compensation, other than being part of the brand story. You might have to consider a form of compensation, but as Guy Kawasaki writes in his 2008 book *Reality Check*,

> I don't advocate paying evangelists. ... However, I recommend kind and frequent gifts of "premiums" or stuff with your logo on it, including t-shirts, bags, mugs, pens, stickers and other gifts. Their monetary

value is visually under $100 but these gifts go a long way with believers.

I'll get more into this in a later chapter. Don't worry.

A WORLD PACKED WITH PUBLISHERS

How Brands Can Make Their Content Stand Out in a Landscape Obsessed with Production

If you've spent any amount of time on social media, you already know the online landscape is flooded with content. As technology has become more and more available, brands now have less control than ever over their audience, and the number of eyeballs viewing their content is dropping quickly. This is, perhaps, a natural result of the amount of competition there now is to attract attention to oneself. Beginning with MySpace, who incentivized users to increase their social standing by having as many online "friends" as possible, social media platforms are now less about connecting with friends and more about collecting influence online. No matter how you feel about the communicative aspects of social media, it is simply impossible to deny that the average user is more concerned with being seen than ever before.

Brands are currently having more trouble than ever connecting with their core audience because, in a way, every user of social media has become a brand of themselves. Users advertise their brand through careful curation of their feeds, walls, and stories with as much loving care and thought as an employee of the MOMA placing pieces in a new exhibit. Whether it's a set of Facebook photos from a night out on the town, a perfectly staged Instagram photo of an elegantly prepared brunch, or a joking tweet sent out to followers in hopes of catching a few shares, nearly every person on the Internet who uses any form of social media, video streaming service, or message board is a publisher producing content. The barrier has been set so low that a world once filled only by those who could invest the time and money into gaining the proper equipment to engage an audience now requires little more than an iPhone, a flashy filter application, and an unlimited data package.

To better illustrate this point, let's take a look at the world of food criticism. For as long as the gourmet world can remember, the key to retaining an audience of diners was the coveted Michelin stars. Gaining one, two, or even three of the coveted stars was a guaranteed way to signal to customers that your food was special, noteworthy, and worth a trip from out of town. Foodies from around the world would wait with bated breath in anticipation to learn which establishments were being awarded stars (or, in other cases, having them taken away) by experts who had tasted the best that the world had to offer. The Michelin star rating system was respected because the food was being reviewed by experts, the best-of-the-best when it comes to palates.

Then came Yelp.com, the consumer review site where anyone could submit a star rating (between one and five) for their favourite restaurants, beauty parlours, and even doctor's offices. Seemingly overnight, the phrase "everyone's a critic" took on a whole new meaning. Thousands of users flooded the site to post reviews of their dining experiences; statistician Nate Silver described the site as "unsophisticated, cheap, and obsessed with trivial details of the restaurant experience."

As the Internet was suddenly overwhelmed with reviews from those who were in no ways gourmets and who spent no time developing their palates or studying flavours, food criticism died almost overnight. Le Bernardin, a three-star seafood restaurant in Manhattan, now holds a lower rating on Yelp than the Halal Guys, a food cart located just around the corner.

In the same way, an endless stream of content is being produced by all social media users, much of which is meaningless and low-quality. This is not a knock to the average social media user; it is impossible to expect a teenager with an iPhone to produce content on par with a brand like Coca-Cola, who has a virtually limitless budget. However, in the flood of content being created, many brands are throwing their media training to the wind and going with an "everything but the kitchen sink" approach to their digital marketing. Instead of carefully creating their content with user intent in mind, they are reposting the same content to Facebook, Twitter, Instagram, Snapchat, TikTok, Twitch, and the like, and running generic ads on every flavour-of-the-week app game that comes to town. This strategy inevitably leads to failure; if brands want to connect with their consumers, they need to do so on a psychological level. Simply gaining eyeballs is not enough.

So what can a brand do to stand out and gain the attention of their customers within a world that's packed to the brim with publishers?

The answer lies in a return to the basic principles of market research. Instead of spreading themselves thin over a number of social media platforms, brands should produce content that is clearly in line with their target audience's values.

Similarly, brands need to develop specific content that is cohesive with each social media platform they select. It is well known that users of Instagram are more focused on visually stimulating, bright, and sight-oriented content. However, fast-food giant Burger King is guilty of cross-posting their same coupons and long-winded captions along with photos of burgers shot from a distance, the same content they regularly upload to their Facebook and Twitter accounts. While the brand could find massive success posting photos of juicy, succulent hamburgers and mouth-watering French fries glistening with salt, they choose to take the quantity-over-quality approach and cross-post their content.

Brands who want to employ an effective digital marketing strategy need to remember that engagement isn't just about getting people to see their content. Nearly every social media outlet now offers sponsorship options, but brands are essentially tossing money out the window every time they purchase an ad on a platform that is incongruent with their audience, or promote a post that's incompatible with a site's landscape. Instead of attempting to spread their presence over as many social media sites as possible, brands should instead focus on creating meaningful content that makes an emotional impact with their target audience.

For example, a fashion brand would benefit from focusing their research on colour psychology to create an Instagram advertisement, while automated mailing service MailChimp would better spend their time researching what types of subreddits they can advertise to in order to increase their click-through rate on Reddit.

Advertisers have a desperate and immediate need to return to quality content. Instead of thinking of the entire landscape of social media users as competition, think of them as potential customers. Know the average user of the social media sites you post to, and create unique, shareable content that is likely to psychologically and emotionally engage native users of the platform. By returning to the quality content, brands can make themselves heard in the endless drone of online content creation.

There is a way to affect these interactions, perceptions, and behaviours, by being true to your brand and your purpose, but again, hold that thought.

In today's media landscape, content has been commoditized, and audience is the new currency.

—Brendan Gahan

CHAPTER 2

PUBLISHERS

Stop Selling and Start Talking

> Just principles conceive just notions and perform
> good actions in consequence of them.
>
> —Hugh Blair

First, let's recap what the definition of *marketing* is; it is the study and management of exchange relationships, meaning the business process of identifying, anticipating, and satisfying what consumers need, want, and desire.

So let's focus a little bit on the consumer, shall we? Are you continually looking for ways to gain credibility with the younger generation? If so, stop lumping all of them into one enormous homogenous generation. Instead, target the specific and distinct groups that make up the younger generation. If you do this, you will have a higher rate of engagement, and millennials just may like you.

There are three tactics that marketers need to use when attempting to reach the right people:

1. Implement the 80/20 Rule in Social Media Marketing

The 80/20 rule will help you gain online credibility with young consumers. In short, 80 per cent of your social media posts need to be about your target customer. The other 20 per cent should be about your company; the majority of your social media posts need to come from reputable sources and be well written. No grammar or spelling mistakes.

The other 20 per cent can be promotional. They need to include a call-to-action, like the following:

- Click to get this great offer.
- Read this article to learn something new.
- Sign up to get a free consultation.
- Grab this code to apply a 20% discount at checkout.

2. Understand the Importance of the 14/78 Rule

The 14/78 rule is connected to understanding and gaining credibility with the audience. Successful marketers know that only 14 per cent of people believe in mainstream media/publishers, and 78 per cent of the younger audience trust the influence of friends and family.

3. Influencer Marketing Is Critical

Influencer marketing focuses on influential people rather than the target market as a whole. Brands looking to target young consumers should concentrate on micro influencers, not celebrities. Real-world influencers are talking to a niche audience but command an equal and sometimes higher engagement rate with their audience. Micro influencers are consumers who have a significant social media following, between 1,000 and 100,000.

Hold that thought.

Go ahead and implement these tactics. Understand the numbers, and execute your marketing plan accordingly. Your ability to reach and gain credibility with young consumers will speak for itself.

The Scale of Credibility

> All credibility, all good conscience, all evidence
> of truth come only from the senses.
>
> —Friedrich Nietzsche

How on earth are marketers and innovators supposed to get their product to the masses when technology is such an oversaturated market? It's not easy, but there is always room for a credible new kid on the block.

The best method to win over the mainstream market is by "crossing the chasm." The idea comes from Geoffrey A. Moore's 2014 book that has become the bible for bringing high tech products to larger markets. If you stick to a single, rigid formula, your technology has a better chance of succeeding.

What Is Crossing the Chasm?

Simply put, a chasm is the difference between people, viewpoints, and feelings. If you hang around high-tech boardrooms or venture capital meetings, you will hear the marketing buzz phrase "crossing the chasm."

If not, this chapter will clarify what it means and explain how to rise above your competition, gain credibility, and reach the masses with your new technology.

The chasm high-tech marketers are talking about is between the Early Adopters and the Early Majority on the Technology Adoption Life Cycle. First, you need to understand the cycle.

The Technology Adoption Life Cycle
Consists of Five Groups of People:

1. **The Innovators.** Innovators love technology. They are enthusiastic about trying new technology, and they aggressively pursue new products. Since technology is central to their life, they are likely to try it, regardless of its functionality.

2. **The Early Adopters.** They also appreciate new technology, especially if it can give their company a competitive advantage in the marketplace. Unlike Innovators, they want to imagine and understand the benefits of new technology in their life or business.

3. **The Early Majority.** This is the bulk of the market and tends to buy into technology once its concept is proven. They are driven by practicality and want to see references before investing.

4. **The Late Majority.** A large part of the market is very conservative in their purchases. They don't buy new technology unless there is solid proof that it's useful.

5. **The Laggards.** These are sceptical buyers who don't buy any new technology unless they absolutely have to. Their lack of interest is sometimes personal and sometimes economic, but overall, they are not worth pursuing.

The basic idea is that there is a chasm between the Early Adopters of the product (the technology enthusiasts) and the Early Majority (the practical buyers).

Marketers need to move the majority of their customers from the Early Adopters to the Early Majority to survive in the oversaturated high-tech market.

How Do We Reach the Early Majority?

Since the Early Majority is the largest part of the market, companies need to understand how they think. The Early Majority buys a product when it's released to the public and when they can read its reviews. They expect new products not only to solve their problems but also to be simple to use. They prefer a more mature product, with better design, more features and integrations, and fewer bugs.

While Early Adopters are willing to sacrifice for the advantage of being first, the Early Majority waits until they know that the technology offers improvements in productivity. The challenge for innovators and marketers is to reach the Early Majority market and gain loyalty while doing so.

1. **Choose a Target Market.** To expand the Early Majority, you need to target a niche market within your field. Pick a market segment that suits your company's ambitions. Getting enough word of mouth recognition will help you become the market leader, which is essential to the Early Majority.

2. **Deliver a Whole Product**. To reach the Early Majority, you will need a complete feature set with all major bugs eliminated. The Early Majority is not as forgiving as early adopters. You also need to make sure that you fulfil the marketing promises you make to your customer.

3. **Create Competition.** Attracting the Early Majority requires competition as a necessary condition for success. They don't want to buy from you unless there are comparable products. It's imperative that you know how to position your product among your competitors. If there is no competition, you are not ready to cross the chasm.

4. **Sell Effectively.** The best way to cross the chasm is through direct sales, as it gives you maximum control over your destiny. Face-to-face meetings help to penetrate the initial target segment. Know your position, and have leadership in place.

5. **Position Yourself Properly.** Position your product between the company currently providing a similar solution and another that delivers an alternative solution. Price yourself in line with products similar to yours, as you are fighting for their current customers. With the second competitor, you need to be prepared to deliver

- two sentences that sell the product,
- clear evidence of leadership,
- communications aimed at the right audience with the correct content at the appropriate time, and
- feedback and adjustment in response to competitor attack.

What Else Can Your Company Do to Cross the Chasm?

Your company can add the following jobs to assist in reaching the Early Majority:

Whole Product Manager. They will be responsible for bringing the product to the mass market by managing the list of bug reports and product improvements. This job will eventually evolve into a product marketing manager once you cross the chasm.

Target Market Segment Manager. This position is responsible for getting the product to the mainstream market. They secure the product in the Early Adopter market segment and put the steps in place to reach the broader market. The target market segment manager is a challenging role that requires creating a bandwagon effect that leads to the product becoming the standard.

Understanding how the Early Majority thinks and following these proven tactics to market to them will help your tech company reach its first steps to full-scale commercialization.

Idea Differentiation Curve

Credibility comes from results. Everything else is just marketing.
—Richie Norton

Beyond the Follower Count: How to Choose a Credible Influencer to Promote Your Product

Influencer marketing has taken over the realm of online advertising. Even if you believe that good old-fashioned word-of-mouth advertising is the best route for your product, there's no way to deny the massive influence that social media success stories have over the world of digital marketing. Influencer marketing involves sponsoring a prominent social media user (usually those with thousands of followers on platforms like Twitter, Instagram, or Facebook) to promote a product in a casual setting. Influencer marketing has gained notoriety over the previous years, thanks to its effectiveness in capitalizing on the traditional effects of word-of-mouth advertising. Unfortunately, effective influencer advertising isn't as simple as choosing a social media user with the largest following and paying them to promote your product. Here are three ways to ensure that you choose an influencer who will effectively connect with potential customers and increase your company's reach:

Know that you get what you pay for. The world of unpaid internships and contributions is quickly coming to an end. Recently, news and thought outlet the Huffington Post announced that they would be ending their unpaid blogging program and begin focusing on narrowing their content by paying for better and more developed contributions. A spokesperson for the platform stated that one of the biggest problems with accepting content from relatively unknown bloggers and writers was the flood of false information and low-quality work. "One of the biggest challenges we all face," company officials said, "in an era where everyone has a platform, is figuring out whom to listen to."

In the same way, businesses and marketers need to understand that large social media influencers charge a hefty price for an endorsement on their channel, page, or account. One of the biggest reasons why brands need to be particularly careful about making the right choice in influencers is because social media users have learned to effectively monetize their posts and often charge large sums of money for a single shout-out.

As a digital marketer, you should be very wary of working with influencers who are willing to promote your products for no charge. While all you will lose is free product, you'll waste more time and money working out which influencers have loyal enough fanbases to be worth sponsoring with product in the first place. You will also have no control over the final message influencers put out to their followers, and you will very rarely receive any form of metrics and data to help your team evaluate the effectiveness of your influencer marketing. Working with micro influencers (social media users with fewer than a hundred thousand followers) is also a huge gamble because these users rarely have data on who their audience is. In the end, the old-fashioned saying is true: you really do get what you pay for.

Choose an influencer with a congruent following. Sure, Kim Kardashian has millions of followers on Instagram and Twitter, but is she right to promote your brand? The risk and reward of effective influencer marketing comes from a carefully crafted balance between paying influencers with larger followings and the higher fees that come along with these contracts. Though an influencer's follower count may be high, a sponsored post featuring your product is worthless if it doesn't result in the influencer's followers going out and purchasing your product. Influencer marketing comes along with no guarantees of future sales; you won't get your money back if the influencer's post does not result in your business recouping its investment. If done correctly, this is not necessarily a bad thing; when compared to traditional avenues of advertising, influencer marketing is a much more genuine way of promoting a product, business, or service. However, if done incorrectly, advertisers are essentially wasting their money.

If you are considering promoting your product through influencer marketing, you should be ready to invest a significant percentage of your time into researching influencers whose message, product specialization, and overall feel of their feed fits with the aesthetic of your brand. One of the biggest mistakes marketers make when entering the world of influencer marketing is judging how effective an influencer's post will be, solely by the follower count and engagement rates that the user boasts. While high follower counts are important when it comes to making your money count and increasing your brand's awareness, a mismatch between the influencer and the brand will come off as inauthentic and destroy the illusion of word-of-mouth advertising that makes sponsored posts so effective.

Before you invest in influencers to promote your product, check out their previous sponsored posts and see if their standard promotions fit with your brand. The best influencer matches are those users who frequently promote products, brands, or services that are related to (but not an exact match of) the product you wish to promote. These types of influencer posts are most likely to be effective because they will seamlessly fit in with the influencer's other sponsored promotions. You should avoid the temptation to sponsor a post with an influencer who is particularly well-known for a sponsorship with an established product that's an exact match with yours. Even if you are able to financially beat out the competing brand, these types of loyalty switch-ups make consumers suspicious and can cause your advertisements to be less effective.

For example, if a beauty blogger has been sponsored by a foundation company for over two years and suddenly switches to a different brand for a few sponsored posts, this can destroy the credibility of the influencer advertising. On the other hand, products that complement foundation (blush, mascara, application sponges, and so on) will be more effective because they work in conjunction with the influencer's established brand, instead of working against it.

Think about your platform. When it comes to influencer marketing, compare your target market and the average user base of the social media platform they operate on. Across social media outlets, there is a very large and divisive gender divide in particular that should be noted by advertisers. For example, on Instagram, a whopping 68 per cent of users are female; advertisers looking to target a female audience will do much better on Instagram than on Reddit, for example, whose audience is 70 per cent male.

Effective influencer advertising lives and dies on the authenticity of the ad. Social media has become such an important tool for advertising because it allows brands to directly connect with their consumers and spur potential new customers to step outside their comfort zones and spend money on a new product or brand. Influencers are the gatekeepers between brands and their audiences; they are the average Joe or Jane the customer feels a connection with, and they treat sponsored posts as personal recommendations with their favourite Internet personalities.

The most important thing advertisers must remember is, they cannot fight against the aesthetic of the influencer, as the sponsored post will come off as inauthentic and a blatant attempt to sell a product. Instead of twisting an influencer to fit your message, put out a call for influencers who fit your brand's message, or change the platform you advertise in. Whether you are targeting teen girls or men in their thirties, there are influencers with massive followings that can help promote your product; you just need to find them.

You Can No Longer Afford to Ignore Influencer Marketing

Influencer marketing has been brewing for about eight years now, and it's currently the go-to tactic for both Business 2 Business (B2B) and Business 2 Consumers (B2C) marketers.

What Is Influencer Marketing?

Influencer marketing focuses on using key people to drive your brand's message to the broader market. Rather than marketing directly to a large group of consumers, you instead hire influencers to get the word out for you.

A 2018 report from BI Intelligence predicted that advertisers will spend between $5 billion and $10 billion in 2022 on influencer marketing. That's big money.

How Do I Get Started in Influencer Marketing?

Chances are, you already engaged in a basic form of influencer marketing. If customers are giving online reviews of your products, or if you are encouraging customers to share their experiences about your brand on social media, you are already in the game.

If it's time to hire professional influencers, you need to create an influencer marketing plan and set some goals. Goals for influencer marketing are often less about driving sales and more about increasing buzz and public awareness.

Here are the four types of influencers you should consider while you set up your influencer marketing plan:

1. **The Influential Educator.** Who doesn't love a good teacher? Educators are helpful and insightful. They have a vast knowledge of a specific topic and are willing to share it with your audience.

2. **The Influential Coach.** A good coach wants you to succeed. Coaches are helpful and focus on continual engagement. A coach will dive deep into LinkedIn discussions or engage in a Twitter conversation because that's what they love to do. Their influence over one's self-determination is huge, and they often give people the push they need to achieve their goals.

3. **The Influential Entertainer.** We love to be entertained. Entertainers are role models with enormous power over people's purchasing decisions. We have all bought a product because our favourite actor or actress spoke highly of it.

   Entertainers are the hardest type of influencer to secure for your campaign because of the price. It can be worth the money, as it could pay off to tap into the audience they command.

4. **The Influential Charismatic.** There is something about a charismatic influencer that works. They tap into the emotional

side of the audience by sharing heart-warming stories, and inspirational messages. They usually have a lot of energy and are skilled at inspiring others.

In addition, we can split the influencer category into two big groups: micro influencers and macro influencers.

When I worked at Ogilvy, we split micro influencers into three subgroups:

1. **Consumer Advocates.** These are the ones who love a brand's product beyond anything (think Apple fans).

2. **Gatekeepers.** These are the people you go to behind a counter for service and advice.

3. **Experts.** These people are considered to know it all within their category.

Macro influencers, with much more of a mass market reach, are divided into two subgroups;

1. **Creators.** These are the YouTubers, the TikTokkers, the SnapChatters: the ones who creates unique content and have a massive following.

2. **Talent.** These are the actors, musicians, and A-list celebrities, the ones who are admired for their fame and fortune, with a massive following, such as Kylie Jenner and Zac Efron.

What Is the Main Challenge with Influencer Marketing?

There is not enough measurement going on. There are insane amounts of money being spent, but not much is known about the return on investment (ROI). This is because marketers cannot yet measure the direct financial return of using influencer marketing.

Here are some tips to tackle this problem:

- Give influencers a unique URL their followers can use so you can easily measure the conversions they drive.
- Measure the ROI by considering other ways influencers might help you achieve your goal. You may be able to measure the campaign according to factors such as traffic driven, social reach, social media impressions, and engagement rate. If the numbers look good, you can assume the influencers did their job.
- Use a tool such as NeoReach, which measures the number of impressions and level of engagement generated by your influencers.

With that said, measuring engagement is your best bet. According to Linqia's *State of Influencer Marketing 2018*, they predicted that 90 per cent of brands measure the success of their influencer marketing campaigns by measuring engagement, not product sales or conversions.

How Do We Keep Influencers Happy?

For Influencers to feel worthwhile and stay interested, they need to be part of the brand, product, and service. When influencers feel included, they will work to be a credible and authentic voice for your product.

The *BI Intelligence Report* highlights ways to build this relationship:

- Brands need to provide influencers with enough creative freedom, while also ensuring the messaging reflects the brand in a positive way (40 per cent of influencers don't like restrictions in their messaging).

- Build a long-term relationship with the influencer, not a one-off. In marketing, one-offs rarely help the long-term impact on the brand.

- Realize their value. The average influencer engagement rate across industry verticals is 5.7 per cent on Instagram. As a comparison, the average engagement rate for brands on Instagram has fluctuated between 2 to 3 per cent.

- Be nice back. Influencers will be providing value to you, but you need to give them value in return. Share their content with your online community, follow their social media channels, and comment on their posts.

- Ask what they think. Stay on top of what your Influencers are saying about your products. Ask them what they think can be improved. An engaging in ongoing dialogue will help to build a trusting relationship.

B2B/B2C

Getting the Attention of Your Tribe. Should B2B and B2C Brands Do Things Differently?

> Knowledge comes by taking things apart: analysis.
> But wisdom comes by putting things together.
> —John A. Morrison

As we dig deeper into attention marketing, I want to address a common marketing quandary: Should B2B and B2C brands try to get attention from their tribes differently?

The short answer is no, not really. There isn't a big difference on how to grab consumers' attention, but you should understand how various marketing principles apply to B2B and B2C brand marketing.

What Is Attention Marketing?

As a reminder, the way brands keep our attention is called attention marketing. The key for marketers is to understand how it works and implement strategies that satisfy the demands of modern consumers, regardless of what they are buying.

What Are the Similarities between B2B and B2C Attention Marketing?

They both need to be authoritative. B2B and B2C marketers both struggle with lead generation and conversion, and that is becoming more difficult as customers have shorter attention spans.

In the past, it was only B2C content that needed to educate and come from a place of authority. The authority or sales rep tirelessly worked to connect with prospects emotionally. The goal was to build lasting corporate relationships. Buying decisions were made based on factual information they could convey to their colleagues, and many people were part of the decision-making process.

There was less pressure for B2C marketers until influencer marketing burst onto the scene. Currently, consumers relate much more positively to people over brands. They want to hear from influential people before making purchasing decisions.

In fact, in a report by Nielsen Global Trust in Advertising, 83 per cent of online respondents in sixty countries say they trust the recommendations of friends and family before any other type of advertising medium.

Businesspeople are people too, as I say in my keynotes on stage around the world. B2B and B2C prospects are both humans. They are subject to the same emotional triggers, and they listen to the same authoritative and trustworthy voices when making buying decisions.

They both need regular engagement. B2B and B2C prospects both need some handholding, as attention spans grow shorter. Sure, the B2B sales cycle is much longer. A sales rep must authentically connect with more people over a more extended period, but B2C customers need love too.

B2B and B2C prospects both need nurturing and high-touch interaction. This tactic will establish long-term and repeat customers.

They both need to communicate. Making communication a priority is an excellent way to get the attention of B2B and B2C consumers. More focus tends to go into the communication process with B2B interactions.

B2B prospects expect clear timelines and require a responsive and flexible sales team during the buying cycle. Depending on the size of the contract, the B2B prospect will expect several phone calls, emails, and video conferences with various levels of lower and upper management.

While B2C consumers don't require the same amount of communication, they do have high standards when it comes to keeping their attention. Marketers must be able to respond quickly to any questions posed via email or social media.

A report from Ambassador says that 71 per cent of online customers expect a response from a brand within five minutes after reaching out on social media. If they don't hear back, 41 per cent say they will leave the site.

Marketing Principles Remain the Same

As brands work to get the attention of their tribes, B2B and B2C marketing principles don't differ in the current market.

All brands need to attract, nurture, and convert their leads by identifying, anticipating, and satisfying their wants and needs. When a team of marketers gathers around a table, they should be answering the following questions, regardless of the brand:

1. What makes our business, product, or service unique? Both B2B and B2C brands need to communicate what sets them apart from the competition.

2. Are we delivering fresh, relevant content? B2B and B2C brands need new content that addresses prospect needs during the buying cycle. It should be designed to keep the attention of the consumer.

3. Is our content building trust? B2B and B2C content should elicit an emotional response from the prospect. The content should be designed to create brand recognition and trust.

4. Are we equipped to address questions and monitor social media conversations quickly? Show that you are listening. Your sales or customer service teams need to be highly responsive to any inquiries. A lapse in communication can lead to losing the attention of your tribe.

5. Are we reaching the right audience? B2B and B2C marketers need to know where their prospects are hanging out to get their attention. LinkedIn is the place to be for the B2B marketplace, while Instagram and Facebook may be better for the individual consumer.

6. Are we neglecting mobile? Nothing loses a tribe member quicker than a poorly designed mobile experience. It is essential for B2B and B2C brands to present a rich mobile platform.

    A Think with Google report called "The Changing Face of B2B Marketing" says that B2B customers are using mobile devices to research products and services. Almost half of B2B researchers who use their mobile devices to examine products do so at work. They're comparing prices, reading about products, comparing feature sets, and contacting retailers. Almost a quarter use their mobile phones to make purchases.

7. Are we speaking the same language as our tribe? B2B and B2C marketers need to adjust their tone and voice to be equal to their target audience to get their attention.

Getting the attention of your tribe boils down to meeting the needs of your client, speaking to them in their language, and convincing them that your product or service is the best. The time it takes will vary from B2B to B2C brands, but the goal remains the same.

Attention marketing aims to build ongoing relationships with customers. They need to like you, trust you, and remember you.

Expedients are for the hour, but principles are for the ages.

—Henry Ward Beecher

CHAPTER 3

WELCOME TO BRAND YOU ECONOMICS

So what is the reason for the title of my book, and the substance, takeaways, and value exchange that I want you to grasp after reading this book?

The thing is, and I'm not pointing fingers at you, because I am sure you're not in this category of people (ha ha), but one thing I come across, more often than you would ever imagine, is that most entrepreneurs, start-ups, scale-ups, and so on are focused on one thing, and one thing only: the amazing solution they have come up with, solving the problem they at some point have personally experienced. And from one point of view, that's amazing, because it mostly is driven by passion or the hopes of making a ton of money (goal).

But then, that is also what might be the reason for the level of success or failure. Because they tend to minimize the importance of things that are needed before and after creating or defining the product or service. And I get it (I am a pure born and bred ad man and marketer).

But most entrepreneurs have little to no clue of all the work that's needed before developing a product or service, especially if you want to become a brand with a legacy. Then you have what is needed afterwards.

In some cases, they go to an agency (bravo) to get the much-needed help, but in other cases, limited by budget (or sometimes arrogance), they know someone, a cousin or a friend of a friend, who can fix it, be it a logo, website, app, investor presentation, or what have you.

Even those who seek professional help tend to think it is a walk in the park. I know of companies that think it will take two or three months to have everything that is needed up and running, only to later realize that it takes somewhere from a year to eighteen months, minimum. And, yes, disclaimer: It is very individual and varies from case to case. It's just a personal opinion and generalization.

So what is the reason for this problem or pain point? The reality check, so to speak?

Here five things I have encountered over the past decades:

1. **Lack of foundation**. It's easy to forget to map out your strengths and weaknesses, and I mean real hard talk. It's easy to come up with all the strengths, especially when starting the journey of a company, but knowing the weaknesses is even more important.

2. **Lack of insight**. What are the opportunities and threats? Are market data and target groups showing a real need or just a perceived need? Are your products or services a painkiller or vitamin pill?

3. **Lack of structure**. Know the answers of the innovations cycle: Why (purpose), How, What, Who, When. These stages need to be mapped out and validated based on facts and insight.

4. **Lack of perspective**. What is the longevity, the game plan, growth, goals, and objectives?

5. **Lack of strategy**. Develop guiding principles, the playbook that tells why your brand exists and how you are going to go from point A to Z.

You definitely need to have a strong product or service, but don't forget everything that makes that product stand out, everything that is needed to build a legendary brand.

This is why I am writing this book: to ignite that spark and make you want to take the important steps before, during, and after crafting your product or service.

So let me simplify what *Brand You Economics* actually is and explain what it's all about. It is the study of everything that influences and impacts your brand performance, based on the principles of interactions, perceptions, and behaviours, and how it affects the bottom line.

Let's break down the three words specifically so you get a better understanding and perspective on the landscape before we go into detail of the principles and how to manage this for your company or yourself.

Let's start with the last word first: economics. It's the social science that studies production, distribution, and consumption of goods and services. The principles of economics focus on the behaviours and interactions of economic agents and explain how economies work.

Next, we have brand, which simply put is your perception of a person, company, organization, product, or service. Simply put (I will refer to this later as well), it is your gut feeling about said person, company, organization, product, or service that determines if you are a brand.

And finally, you. Think about it for a second. Today, almost everyone is a content creator, and because of your activities online, people have a perception about you, a gut feeling, so when we as brandividuals or gatekeepers or influencers produce, distribute, and sell our space, we become economic agents. Meaning we become brands. Basically, everyone who is online with the hopes of making money from their time or product or service is a brandividual or influencer. But another dimension is that companies also behave like people online, because the consumer craves more authentic interactions and conversations. So simply put, people behave as brands, and brands behave as people.

Brand You Economics is the science and study of the principles and tangible tools that will help you build a legacy brand. I will focus on these principles throughout this book; the insight and knowledge behind this is timeless. Granted, some of the examples and references are specific, but the ideas, principles, structure, foundation, and strategy are timeless, which means that this book is a tool to be used now and for decades to come.

So let's begin and deep dive into the understanding of why it is important to act as a human, whether you are an individual or a company.

Seven Ways to Humanize Your Brand

Your customers, partners, employees, and social media fans are human, so why is your marketing team still talking to customers like they are robots? Say goodbye to boring corporatespeak and outdated marketing practices, and say hello to *Brand You Economics*. It's time to let the human side of your brand shine.

Hold that thought.

What Is Brand You Economics?

Brand You Economics means that you are your brand, and your brand is you. People no longer trust brands that spew confusing, unrelatable corporate jargon. Today, consumers prefer marketing messages that come from people they feel a connection to.

A report from Forrester revealed that 70 per cent of US adults online trust recommendations from each other far more than statements from brands. So what's the solution? Your marketing team needs to create a brand that seems more like a person. It is a straightforward concept, but the execution can be tricky.

Here are seven tips to help your team get started:

1. **Give your brand a human voice.** It's hard for marketers to assign human qualities to a logo or a corporate name. As you develop the human voice for your brand, your team can create with a fictional character to represent it. They should ask the following questions when envisioning this character:

   - Who is this person?
   - What's their name?
   - How do they dress?
   - What's their favourite food?
   - What are their likes and dislikes?
   - Are they extroverted or introverted?
   - Do they have a formal or casual appearance?

   This tactic will help your team imagine a real person to serve as your brand voice.

2. **Hire a micro influencer to be a voice on your social networks.** You don't need million-dollar celebrity budgets to make an impact. Micro influencers are everyday people who have highly engaged followers around relevant topics. I mentioned before that they can range from 1K up to 100K followers; in this case, I am referring to Gatekeepers, the ones who have between 2K and 25K monthly visitors—and according to Kissmetrics, this

lower visitor count provides a sixteen times higher engagement rate than other paid media alternatives.

Messages from these kinds of micro influencers are perceived as more genuine than many of the big celebrities on Instagram and Pinterest.

3. **Stop scheduling all marketing messages.** This is challenging, as scheduling tools are beneficial for time management. However, they do distance your brand from your audience.

Your marketing team should post casual, personal messages from time to time. It's important to react to things in the moment so your brand will come across as more human. This strategy comes with more pressure and a larger time commitment, but consumers will take notice.

This is especially effective on a platform like Twitter. JetBlue has been extremely successful at interacting with their customers via Twitter in an authentic and relatable way. When you tweet at a company with over sixteen thousand employees, you may not expect a response right away, if at all. However, JetBlue has done a fantastic job differentiating themselves on Twitter by finding clever ways to exceed our expectations.

4. **Talk to your consumers.** This is the era where your brand needs to engage in conversations with customers. Ask them what they like and what they want to see. If they compliment your product, thank them.

If your audience members are commenting on one of your Facebook threads, jump into the discussion authentically. This shows that you're paying attention and that you care about their opinions. The more you engage with your customers, the more likely they'll be to see you as trustworthy and relatable. This does require more work, but you'll grow your customer loyalty considerably.

5. **Show up.** Don't set up the latest social network profile unless you plan to be active on it. There is nothing worse than an inactive brand on social media. Your marketing team needs to understand how to effectively interact with customers before they create a corporate user profile. Show up with a goal to inspire and connect with your audience. Be proactive and responsive.

6. **Be funny.** Humour is one of the key foundations to forming a connection. When we laugh together, we bond with each other. When you make your customers laugh, you are showing them an authentic side of yourself.

   This vulnerability shows your customers that you aren't afraid to set aside the professionalism of your brand to experience a human moment. Your marketing team doesn't need to hire comedy writers, but they should work to post enough humour to keep your audience feeling good about your brand.

7. **Share photos and videos of your team being human.** As you embrace *Brand You Economics*, your marketing team should share human moments with their followers.

   Post photos and videos from your company party. If your group goes to a team-building event, let your followers know ahead of time, and ask them what department they think will do the best. If you have a team meeting, share photos of a brainstorming session. These shares help build a real relationship with the people in your community.

What Is the Goal of Brand You Economics?

The goal of *Brand You Economics* is creating an identity for your customers to interact with. You want to turn your company into something people can relate to, not something cold and impersonal. When customers enjoy your brand identity, they'll want to befriend your personality and will feel more loyal to your brand.

You also want customers to buy into the culture around your brand. They should want to make themselves more like the personality of your brand, which will lead them to purchase more of your product.

It's time to stop thinking like a corporation and start thinking like a person. Humanizing your brand is a requirement if you want to survive in business today. The sooner you adapt to *Brand You Economics*, the sooner you will start building relationships, nurturing friendships, and earning the respect of powerful brand influencers who will elevate you and your company to the next level.

YOU ARE A BRAND

Calling All Brands! It's Time to Become Human

You have to stay true to your heritage; that's what your brand is about.

—Alice Temperley

There is a marketing movement happening that your company can't ignore. Brands no longer want to be seen as intimidating corporate titans. They want to be viewed as companies that value their customers as individuals. While buzzwords like *engagement* and *social* have been popular for a while, the latest trend is for brands just to be human.

This movement is, in part, due to research indicating that 63 per cent of people are influenced more by other people than brands. Simply put, brands need to act like humans to today's consumers.

What's the Challenge for Brands?

Brands are scared. As they venture into the process of humanizing themselves, it's not uncommon for them to feel nervous or fearful of losing control of their messaging. In fact, only 3 per cent of brands have started marketing themselves on a personal level. This leaves tons of opportunity for your marketing team, but first, you have to get started.

What Are the First Steps for Marketing Teams?

First, marketing teams should be prepared to promote the importance of brand personalization with management. According to a study by Epsilon Research, 80 per cent of consumers are more likely to do business with a company they feel a personal connection to.

Next, they have the giant task of figuring out how to update their marketing tactics so their brands stay relevant. Brands need to focus on marketing that engages individual consumers, based on their unique interests and preferences.

How Do Companies Get Started in Brand Humanization?

A great way to start is to slowly implement into your marketing strategy what I call the three Cs of attention marketing: Culture, Context, and Community.

Culture. Start to produce content in line with the culture of your brand and the audience you want to reach. Become part of a cultural conversation that is relevant to your brand. Don't be afraid to hijack existing cultural moments to prove you are in touch with what is happening at the moment.

Align your brand story with the needs and interests of your audience. Make sure your brand is organically woven into the content narrative and speaks in a tone that resonates with consumers.

For example, women's empowerment has been a large part of the cultural conversation over the past several years, and brands are responding.

The campaign #LikeAGirl from Always and Under Armour's "I Will What I Want" have been paramount in redefining the role of women in sports to one of strength and empowerment.

Context. This refers to delivering the right kind of message, at the right time, to the right person. It's tough to do this well, but it's becoming increasingly important to hold the attention of your audience.

For example, Cracker Barrel is now using highly targeted messaging strategies. This includes creative messaging on various online media platforms. One example is a micro-targeted and highly personalized integrated campaign called "The Office Hero" that supports their business-to-business, meal-catering program.

When you add context to your relationship with a potential customer, you can provide personalized marketing content that's targeted to their needs. When done right, you will avoid producing the kind of marketing that annoys people.

Community. Developing a community of consumers is imperative in today's marketplace. The most effective marketers can rely on their community instead of paid media. A community is a two-way conversation that is extremely interactive and social. Some people still just watch or read, but many will participate and share your content with their friends. A few things to consider:

1. **Be present** with your target audience. Develop a regular exchange that will create trust. Live up to the expectations you create.

2. **Be responsive**. Listen and be positive. Engage and involve your audience by asking them to share your content. Produce material that is worth sharing, and make sure it's easy to do.

3. **Leverage** fans to amplify your brand. Your customers and followers can be an extension of your marketing team. Give them the tools so they can talk about your brand. Participation will lead to amplification.

A brand that has been very successful at building community is Sony's PlayStation. They have done an exceptional job at providing an online space for gamers to connect by game, interests, or the type of support they need. The brand uses feedback, advocacy, and superior customer service to keep their customers engaged.

PlayStation also promotes user-generated content. Starting with the PS4, users could upload in-game clips directly online. This move will increase the strength of the community and enable it to grow.

The Importance of Brand Storytelling

In the past, marketers could create compelling images, add a memorable tagline, and then push their message out through mass media. It was simplistic, but it worked. Now, brands need to break through the clutter by becoming master storytellers to keep the attention of their audience.

Humans have long been charmed by stories. Stories make us stand in line to see a movie, rush home to watch our favourite TV show, and keep our eyes glued to our mobile devices. A great story holds our attention and makes us want to see more.

Telling your story is a critical part of building your brand. It shapes how people view you and enables consumers to form a connection with you and your company. When done right, you will develop a thriving brand with people who love what you do, what you stand for, and the stories you tell.

Examples of Successful Brand Storytelling

Minnetonka uses storytelling to promote a family brand that supplies products that look good, are comfortable, and will last. They use stories that transcend class and generations. They have a company history on their website which is presented as a short timeline and ends with an inspirational movie that delves into the brand's beliefs and its relationship with its consumers.

In 2017, Nike's "Equality" campaign used storytelling to celebrate differences and inspire change through the power of sport. Nike launched the campaign with a moving video that asked us to extend the respect we see on the court, rink, or field into the real world. The campaign included a line of athletic apparel and plans to donate $5 million to US charities dedicated to equality.

It's time for your company to move away from impersonal marketing messaging and evolve into a modern brand that consumers feel a personal connection with. Gather up your team, and brainstorm ways to link your brand to broader cultural movements. Build an engaged community, and target different consumers with unique messages. Use excellent storytelling to connect people to your brand.

The Brand Is You

When people use your brand name as a verb, that is remarkable.

—Meg Whitman

Influencer Marketing Has Been Around Longer Than You Think

I've described the enormous power of influencer marketing, identified the four types of influencers commonly hired by marketers, and described their value in today's marketplace.

Let's dig deeper into the history of influencer marketing. After all, marketers and advertisers have been using influencers long before DJ Khaled burst onto the social media scene.

What Is Influencer Marketing?

As a reminder, influencer marketing focuses on using key people to drive your brand's message to the broader market. Rather than marketing directly to a large group of consumers, you instead hire influencers to get the word out for you.

Influencers speak passionately about a topic. They are connoisseurs who can influence others about the issues they talk about. They have a community interested in what they say and what they do, write, and publish.

When Did Influencer Marketing Begin?

Despite popular belief, influencer marketing didn't start with the launch of Facebook, Twitter, and YouTube. The act of using highly influential individuals to endorse consumer goods and services has been around for hundreds of years.

There was a study in 1940 entitled "The People's Choice" by Lazerfeld & Katz that looked at political communication. It concluded that the majority of people are influenced by second-hand information.

Examples of Influencer Marketing before Social Media

In the 1930s, Coca-Cola used the charm of Santa Claus to sell soda. In the 1950s, the Marlboro Man sold cigarettes, and in the 1980s, Mary Lou Retton was the first woman athlete featured on a Wheaties box.

So What's Different Now?

The difference is that the current marketing influencers are much more humanized, approachable, and accessible than ever before. They are not all celebrities, and some would argue that micro influencers are even more powerful than celebrity influencers.

In the past, there were no social media platforms to elevate the voices of influencers. Celebrities did not interact with consumers, and micro influencers had little (if any) impact.

The Tipping Point **Started It All**

Malcolm Gladwell was a pioneer in writing about influencer marketing. In 2000, his book *The Tipping Point* became an international bestseller.

In the book, Gladwell describes the Law of the Few:

> There are exceptional people out there who are capable of starting epidemics. All you have to do is find them.

Gladwell identified three different types of influencers in his book: Connectors, Mavens, and Salespeople. These influencers remain relevant in influencer marketing tactics more than twenty years later.

The Connectors. The connectors are people who know everybody. They have a vast network of friends and colleagues, and they're instrumental in spreading the word. These individuals are confident, energetic, and social, and they have the innate ability to befriend people with a wide range of views.

In today's world of influencer marketing, a connector would have a lot of friends on Twitter. A connector might also have a podcast. They build a deeper relationship with their network by finding new guests, which often come by way of introduction from past guests.

The Mavens. These are the experts in a particular subject matter. They are the computer nerds, the movie buffs, or the fashion-forward friends. The mavens are the people you ask first when you need advice or help.

According to a study done at Clarkson University entitled "Connectors, Mavens, Salesmen and More: An Actor-Based Online Social Network (OSN) Analysis Method Using Tensed Predicate Logic," mavens are information gatherers who pass along information to many people. They like to continually share their information with many individuals until it becomes a social epidemic.

The Salespeople. These are the charismatic people who persuade others to jump on board. Their charm and gift of gab appeal to different types of people.

In today's world of influencer marketing, salespeople are those we follow on Snapchat or Instagram. They are highly entertaining and inspirational, with great personalities. They possess the ability to excite us, and they can sell us anything.

Influencer Marketing Facts

No matter how you define influencers, the following influencer marketing facts from tapinfluence.com cannot be ignored:

- Influencer marketing content delivers 11x higher ROI than traditional forms of digital marketing.
- Twitter users report a 5.2x increase in purchase intent when exposed to promotional content from influencers.
- 74% of people turn to social networks for guidance on purchase decisions.
- 40% of people say they've purchased an item online after seeing it used by an influencer on Instagram, Twitter, TikTok, or YouTube.
- Teens' emotional attachment to YouTube stars is 7x greater than their traditional celebrities.
- Among teens, YouTube stars are perceived as 17x more engaging and 11x more extraordinary than mainstream stars.

- 71% of marketers believe that ongoing ambassadorships are the most effective form of influencer marketing.

Why Is Influencer Marketing So Popular Today?

The rise of social sharing platforms like Instagram, Snapchat, and YouTube means that users can build up their followings by sharing in-the-moment stories and posting about their day-to-day lives.

We Are Only Human

Also, consumers are overloaded with messages both online and offline. As technology overtakes the amount of daily human interactions, our natural need for connection is driving us to listen to influencers over brands when it comes to our behaviour.

Social media platforms allow us to build relationships with people who appeal to us. When people build up their followings in places like Instagram and Snapchat, they also develop trust with their followers. This bond means that their followers are more likely to listen to what they say.

It takes 20 years to build a
reputation and five minutes to
ruin it. If you think about that,
you'll do things differently.

—Warren Buffett

CHAPTER 4

SMALL WORLD

Interactions: The First Principle of Brand You Economics)

**Three Pixels of Separation: Marketing
to Anyone, Anywhere, Anytime**

It has become such a small world. Marketers can now talk to anyone, anywhere, anytime.

Just a couple of decades ago, I couldn't imagine being connected and mutually followed by the owner and curator of TED (@TEDChris), or even be tweeting with a famous actress (@Alyssa_Milano) or, even more crazy, the former president of the United States (@BarackObama), which means anyone, anywhere, anytime can get in touch with one another.

The ability to talk to anyone, anywhere, anytime transformed the principle of six degrees of separation. In 2009, Mitch Joel wrote a book called *Six Pixels of Separation*. The book describes how we no longer live in a world of six degrees of separation, but rather a world where we exist on six pixels of separation.

This concept changes everything we know about doing business. The book presented a complete set of tactics, insights, and tools to enable you to expand your consumer base and reach a global audience.

Three Pixels of Separation Is Where We Are At

Since the book was published in 2009, I feel we are now connected by only three pixels of separation. We are more than ever interlinked through many online platforms. A digital platform refers to the software or hardware of a site. For example, Facebook, LinkedIn, Yelp, Instagram, and Twitter are all digital platforms.

The challenge is establishing and maintaining authentic relationships across this ever-expanding list.

Do Authentic Relationships Even
Mean Anything Anymore?

Yes, more than ever. Marketers must navigate the never-ending list of platforms to meet customers, where they must ensure the messages they put out are both genuine and in alignment with their brand. They need to do this while competing to showcase their products and services in an appealing light. It's not easy, but it's possible.

What Challenges Are Connected to Building
Authentic Digital Relationships?

One challenge is that marketers need to be experts in building trust, as customers equate trust with brand loyalty and authenticity. Nielsen Research posted a study about trust in advertising. When asked what advertising sources they trusted most, 83 per cent of people said, "Someone I know," and 66 per cent said, "Opinions posted online." Catchy taglines and memorable jingles are a thing of the past. Marketers need to learn how to hone in and connect with customers in the digital world.

Another challenge is that even though we live in a highly digitized state, people still form better relationships in the real world than in the virtual world. Marketers must get smart about building digital relationships that translate into real-world experiences.

How Can We Be Good Digital Citizens and Connect to Our Customers Authentically?

Get real. In 2009, Domino's Pizza responded to a video two of its employees uploaded to YouTube. The video filmed a prank in one of the stores and reached over one million views before being taken down. Rather than a traditional press release apology, the company released a YouTube comeback in which the president of the company owned up to their mistakes, apologized, and announced new hiring practices. They also started a Twitter account to respond directly to complaints.

This was a case where a company used digital channels to address a major crisis in a real way, and it paid off considerably, improving the overall brand trust and perception.

Be more than a sale. The sales cycle no longer ends with a purchase. Take Amazon as an example. For millions around the world, Amazon is the trusted name in e-commerce, because they go beyond just sending you what you ordered. They easily offer replacements, refunds, and recommendations. Their marketing doesn't stop after a transaction.

Be online. Good digital citizens will have an online presence all the time. Employees will know the latest platforms, understand how the platform is being used, and be aware of who is using them. Whoever is in charge of online marketing needs to show respect for customers, regardless of who they are. They need to be respectful and positive, and in the case of any negative correspondence, they cannot overreact.

This employee should take the time to see what other companies are doing online and update management accordingly. They need to analyse these competitors properly and be savvy enough to reject what is wrong for your brand. It's important to explore the many opportunities in the digital world and embrace new technology.

Do not spam. You should never spam your customers, as it's annoying, seems dishonourable, and is inauthentic. If you are posting content on social media platforms all day long, it isn't considered promotion anymore; it's called spamming. If you are posting content from morning to night on Facebook, Twitter, Pinterest, and LinkedIn, your customers will consider you a spammer and disregard your messages.

Be empathetic. Becoming a genuinely empathetic brand starts with talking to the people you hope to influence so you understand where you can have the biggest impact on their lives. Brands should develop content that evokes empathy because when they do, consumers are more likely to take action. They will share, respond, and even take part in change within their communities.

When building empathy, here are some questions to ask your customers:

- What do you struggle with the most?
- What are you most afraid of?
- How can we help you?

According to YouTube stats, people are actively seeking out content that prompts a change in themselves and world around them. Procter & Gamble expressed its empathy in its "Thank You, Mom" campaign by depicting the struggles that come along with parenthood.

The ad, which was released in time for the 2012 London Olympics, shows mothers in different locations and their difficulties in raising young athletes. By evoking empathy for the mothers, viewers could connect to the story, making the sporting successes of their Olympian children all the more powerful.

Now that our world is only separated by three pixels of separation, marketers must most make the most out of the various ways they can reach anyone, anytime, anywhere. The most important brands of today successfully reach mass audiences, one individual at a time, with communications that create emotional experiences while being respectful digital citizens.

DIVING INTO CUSTOMER JOURNEY MAPPING THE EASY WAY

The Customer Journey

It's safe to say that a brand or company's success is directly linked to their relationship with their customers. How you deal with your customer's mindset before, during, and after a transaction is essential; strategy is needed to positively influence their behaviour.

Companies that thrive and survive are those where the customer is at the heart and focus of the strategy. Every touchpoint needs to be about delighting the customer with a positive experience. The best brands use customer journey mapping (CJM) to get this done right.

CJM is important for B2C and B2B brands. B2B brands can especially benefit, as their clients are often larger and more complicated; they usually have a purchase process that stretches over a longer timeline.

Customer Journey Mapping Helps You Understand the Consumer Process

What Is Customer Journey Mapping?

Customer journey mapping helps marketers outline the story of a customer's experience from the first interaction with their business to a long-term relationship. It is created from the client's point of view.

I'm sure your team has considered using customer journey mapping in the past, but it likely gets pushed to the back-burner. Truthfully, it can be complicated and intimidating, but it doesn't have to be.

I strongly advise you to start customer journey mapping ASAP. The only way to improve your relationship with your customer is to know where your customers are and where they are going.

Every buyer persona you create, every ad you promote, every landing page you publish, and every email you send out should encourage customers to act, while predicting and preparing for the action they are likely to take next.

You want your customers to like what they see and take action. Or else you want them to love the experience so much that they gladly share it with their friends and family through word of mouth and social media.

Who Is Involved in CJM?

Customer journey mapping should always be a collaborative process. Brand managers, marketers, and customers are ideally included in this activity. This approach gives your team a full perspective on what goes on, from the moment a customer discovers your brand up to the purchase stage.

What Does CJM Look Like?

All maps are different, and there are numerous examples all over the Internet that suit different brands.

Here is an example of customer journey mapping. This map is designed to show customer touchpoints. Touchpoints are the ways consumers experience your product or service. It can be through websites, retail stores, email, social media, mobile apps, and so on. Every one of these touchpoints presents a valuable opportunity to engage with your customers, listen to what they say, and use their feedback to optimize the customer journey.

What Are the Advantages of Creating Customer Journey Maps?

1. **Get valuable insights.** Customer journey mapping gives marketers a peek into customer expectations at each step of their journey. This will help you create experiences that motivate customers to reach the last point of the journey. Any distinct point where customers interact with the organization should be part of a customer journey map.

2. **Understand customer expectations.** Customer journey maps allow you to understand the channels and touchpoints your customers are likely to take to get to your product, what expectations they have for your product, and what their possible frustrations could be.

   For example, when you buy a car, a major touch is taking a test drive or sitting down at the salesperson's desk to negotiate the final deal. Minor touchpoints might be when the customer walks around the lot before being greeted by a salesperson.

3. **Predict and influence consumer behaviour.** A detailed customer journey map, informed by the right data, helps you predict and therefore change customer behaviour, which in turn optimizes the conversion process.

What Components Should Be Included in a Customer Journey Map?

Don't rush. Yes, your brand needs to get on this, but not all customer journey maps are created equal. Some are much more effective at telling the customer's story than others. Great journey maps combine storytelling and visualization so teams can understand and address customer needs. While maps take a wide variety of forms depending on context and business goals, certain elements are generally included.

Here are five elements that your team should incorporate as you begin the process of creating journey mapping:

1. **Timeline.** Customer journey maps are diagrams that visualize the actions, thoughts, and feelings of a person or group over time. It's important to keep your timeline simple. I suggest a timeline that runs from left to right across the middle of the page.

2. **Customer steps.** The map should show what the customer is doing at all times. Examples include researching phones online, trying shoes on at a store, or having coffee with their sales rep. These steps should be written from the perspective of the customer.

3. **Customer profile.** A business executive and a group of guys planning a fishing trip are going to have very different needs and experiences when booking a flight or a hotel. Each journey

map should represent the experience of one and only one persona. The journey map should include the customer's name, age, location, and a few behaviours that will help your team understand why this customer experiences the journey as she or he does. Customer photographs will also bring them to life.

4. **Customer emotion.** Including the emotional state of your customers at each stage allows your team to assess whether your marketing messages are being delivered in the best way.

5. **Supporting evidence.** Data points will help your team understand the customer journey at a deeper level. Customer history, quotes, and research will add a deeper level of understanding. Studying customer insights helps you discover what they think, feel, and go through as they interact with your organization, from beginning to end.

Customer journey maps are essential and help make sure the customer experience is hassle-free. If the path to conversion is organized and straightforward for customers, they're less likely to abandon a brand.

To accomplish great things, we must not only act, but also dream, not only plan, but also believe.

—Anatole France

CHAPTER 5

TOUCHPOINTS (BEHAVIOURS)

Find (Strangers)

Why Finding the Right Tribe Will Help Your Business Thrive

Humans want to fit in. We are social animals that possess a number of behaviours that motivate us towards being part of a larger group. The feeling of wanting to fit in, or be part of a tribe, is something we all can relate to, as it gives us a sense of purpose.

As a marketer, you need to know how to find your tribe. Then, when you've found your tribe, you need to know how to trigger the desired response in them. Marketers need to understand what drives their tribe members and also what stops them.

Does this sound hard? It is hard, and it takes a lot of work, but it's a critical step in finding new customers that will help drive your business.

Fortunately, thanks to the Internet, it's easier than ever for new tribes to form. It's also easier for people to be a part of many tribes because information is so much more accessible.

A Brilliant Example of Tribe Building

In 1997, Apple launched the "Think Different" ad campaign. This ad brilliantly addressed existing members of the Apple tribe, while also recruiting millions of new members to the brand. The fact is, millions of people heard this copy and immediately wanted to be part of the Apple tribe:

> Here's to the crazy ones. The misfits. The rebels. The troublemakers. The round pegs in the square holes.
>
> The ones who see things differently. They're not fond of rules. And they have no respect for the status quo. You can quote them, disagree with them, glorify or vilify them.
>
> About the only thing you can't do is ignore them. Because they change things. They invent. They imagine. They heal. They explore. They create. They inspire. They push the human race forward.
>
> Maybe they have to be crazy.
>
> How else can you stare at an empty canvas and see a work of art? Or sit in silence and hear a song that's never been written? Or gaze at a red planet and see a laboratory on wheels?
>
> We make tools for these kinds of people.
>
> While some see them as the crazy ones, we see genius. Because the people who are crazy enough to think they can change the world, are the ones who do."

Your Tribe Means Everything to Your Business

Okay. Not everyone has the marketing team that Apple has, so you will likely need some help. Remember that your customers, people, squad, or target audience are the most important group of humans in your life (I'm referring to your business life, of course).

They are the lifeblood of your business, and you need to know who they are, how they spend their day, if they are married or single, what phone and apps they use, and what stereotypes they fall into.

This knowledge will drive your entire marketing strategy from the product and promotion to the pricing. It's not always easy to get to know your audience, and it inevitably takes more than an hour or two to gather around a whiteboard.

Questions to Ask Your Marketing Team as You Define Your Tribe

What are the needs, desires, and plans of our target audience?

What are we most knowledgeable about so we can fully engage with our audience?

Which channels are we comfortable with? For example, determine if you're skilled at producing videos to entertain your audience or should use Twitter to amplify your message. Find where your team is most comfortable and knowledgeable, and respond to these questions in their area.

How to Find Your Tribe

Taking the time to find your tribe will help you to not waste precious resources, like time, money, and personnel. This is not a straightforward process; it sometimes requires help from outside resources. The following steps will get you on your way:

1. **Define your niche.** Who are the people you are most passionate about regarding your business? Define them, and bring them your A game in marketing. Your energy and passion will shine through and make you appealing to the specific audiences you seek.

2. **What do you want from them?** This needs to be clearly defined. Is your goal for them to buy one product from you or many? Do you want them to share content or read your newsletter? What is the one thing you want to change about their behaviour? This will help you define your tribe on an even deeper level.

3. **Know your competition.** It's essential to know how your competition engages their audience and communicates their messages. You can always learn from them and adapt your strategy, if necessary. Also, be aware of what new innovations are happening in your category or niche.

4. **Listen.** In marketing, this is often the most underestimated word of all. Start simple by defining basic demographics of your target audience, but then move on to psychographics. Listen and learn what their interests, hobbies, and passions are. Listen to what they do in their spare time with their extra money. Learn about their favourite movies, TV shows, and Internet channels. The more you know about them, the more you can meet their needs and solve their problems.

5. **Attract gatekeepers.** Work hard to find the influencers who are active in your niche. If they like you, they will grant you access to their tribe and you will be one step closer to success.

6. **Keep your audience profile up to date.** Revisit and optimize this list every six to twelve months to make sure you are on target.

When you are ahead of the curve and know precisely who your tribe is, your product, pricing, promotions, and marketing positioning will be more on point. You will be able to define the audience you hope to influence and determine what behavioural changes you'd like to see in them.

If you cannot connect to your tribe and solve their problems, your business will likely fail. Harsh, but true. Yes, this is a lot of work, and you might require external help, but it is well worth it in the end.

LIKE (CUSTOMERS)

Creating a Positive Customer Experience in Three Steps

In the last chapter, we talked about finding your tribe and identifying your ideal customer. Now that you have worked hard to find your tribe, it's time to get their attention, engage with them, and make them like your business. Creating an unforgettable customer experience will do just that.

According to_*The 2016 State of Marketing Report* from HubSpot, marketing has now entered the age of the customer. They have more information and power at their disposal than ever before. We, the marketers, must rise to meet their expectations and offer better buying experiences.

Customer Engagement Plays a Huge Role in a Positive Customer Experience

In the past, brand awareness and success meant a one-way B2C broadcast. Today, it is all about customer engagement. The importance of personal relationships with two-way communication, dialogue, and social conversations is essential for brand awareness and success.

Think about the brands and products you like most. Most likely, it is less about the cost or convenience and more about product appeal and customer experiences, am I right?

We all know what a good customer experience looks like from our own perspective. These good experiences are often emphasized when bad experiences occur.

To quote Jeff Bezos from Amazon, "If you make a customer unhappy, they won't tell five friends, they'll tell five thousand friends."

Three Steps to Create a Positive Customer Experience

1. **Identify.** Now it's time to map out and identify the ideal customer experience. What does an optimal experience look like? Start by mapping out everything your customer does during the engagement with your brand, services, or products. Be sure that you include actions and tasks.

   You will want to study your customer's behaviour across the entire user experience. Personas, interviews, observation, and surveying may be used in this step.

   Next, try to predict what your tribe members are thinking and feeling when they engage with your business. Emotion is the most important thing in the customer experience; they are making emotional decisions to do business with you, not do business with you, refer you, or leave you.

   It may feel slightly uncomfortable for you to try and think about this touchy, feely part, or to try and guess what your customers are thinking and feeling, but it is essential in determining the ideal customer experience.

Assign an emotion to how you want them to feel every step of the way. Don't say "good" or "happy," as those are not deep enough emotions to truly engage and connect with your customer.

Do you want them to feel relieved? Cared for? Do you want them to look for the positive in a bad situation? Now think about what kind of small moments in the journey will help them feel that way.

Once your team has gathered all the information, you can assess the positive and negative aspects of their customer experience. From here, your team can map out the ideal customer experience for your tribe members.

2. **Set concrete objectives.** Once you know what success looks like in the eyes of your customer, you need to turn it into functions and stages. You need to create processes that represent and intensify the total customer experience.

If your brand promises convenience, then make everything about your experience as convenient as possible. If you are promising to overcome an obstacle, then make sure every part of the customer experience helps your customers solve their problems.

Don't offer customer perks to only new customers. If you do this, you could be missing the perfect opportunity to create lasting and meaningful relationships with those who are potential advocates for your business. Create ways to say thank you and reward the most loyal of your tribe members.

Setting concrete objectives will move prospects logically along the path of becoming a customer, to the point where they are so thrilled, they automatically become advocates and referral sources.

3. **Make them a reality.** Once these objectives are identified and objectified, it's time to reverse-engineer the funnel. Address each action to the right person or department, meaning get input from those involved in creating the customer experience.

    You can have the most detailed and insightful customer funnel, but if you don't have engaged employees to deliver it, the customer experience is very likely to fail along the way.

    Richard Branson believes this passionately, which is why he makes sure that Virgin has some of the most vocal brand advocates in the world. He has said, "The way employees are treated is the way they will treat your customers."

    Have your market research team measure and interpret data. They should be able to measure the success of many aspects of your customer experience plan.

    It's essential to create a set of metrics that point to the success or failure of your business. Steady growth in these metrics can help you determine if the customer experience plan is succeeding.

    They can measure the customer experience by monitoring granular things, such as the number of testimonials on Facebook, or the number of newsletters that are opened each month in an email.

    If you operate a retail store, get feedback from your employees who are face to face with customers every day. Are they executing the objectives you requested when you mapped out the ideal customer experience? Are they greeting customers in a polite, nonaggressive way? Do they have several touchpoints with customers while they are in the store? Are they authentic when they engage with shoppers?

Employees who work on the front line of your business, such as those operating the call centres, responding to social media comments, and picking up on sales leads, have the most in-depth knowledge of your customer base. A systematized employee feedback program is a useful way to gain their insights.

More and more successful businesses are coming to understand the marketing success that occurs when they create a rich customer experience. The goal is to connect with customers emotionally so they will talk about your business with everyone they know.

While it's important to have great products and services, it's probably not enough in 2021 and beyond. You will need to wrap great products and services in a total customer experience that keeps them coming back for more.

LOVE (FRIENDS)

Three Ways to Shrink the Customer Experience Gap

The days of being successful by offering a differentiated product are over. Ultimate success now comes when you make customers feel as if they are part of your family. You want them to feel the love for your brand/product/company and then share that love with their personal and professional circles.

For today's consumer, shopping is shopping, plain and simple. What they expect is to feel valued, appreciated, and loved by you. Many businesses understand the importance of this concept, but there remains a dissonance between theory and practice.

What Is the Customer Experience Gap?

The customer experience gap is the difference between what customers expect and what they experience, across industries and commercial channels. The truth is, many industries in the B2B and B2C marketplaces are significantly behind the level of service, speed, and overall shopping experience expected by modern consumers.

Now more than ever, you need a world-class customer experience. With Amazon leading the way in the disruption of B2C retail, the customer shopping experience is forever changed.

Let's face it; you have your work cut out for you when Amazon offers personalized, one-click purchasing, free shipping, and same-day delivery.

How Do You Close the Customer Experience Gap?

If you want customers to rave about your company and give you lots of love, you have to focus on improving the following three areas of your business:

1. Employee engagement. Improving employee engagement is highly correlated with improving customer experience and profitable growth.

According to a report from the Temkin Group, highly engaged employees are more than four times as likely to recommend the company's products and services and do something good for the company that is not expected of them.

Also, engaged employees are 2.5 times as likely to stay at work late if something needs to be done after the normal workday ends, and seven times as likely to recommend that a friend or relative apply for a job at their company.

The problem is that most companies are failing to engage and inspire their workforce. According to the data company Gallup, only 31.5 per cent of the US workforce consider itself engaged in work. (In its study, Gallup defines engaged employees as those who are involved in, enthusiastic about, and committed to their work and workplace.)

How to Engage Employees

How to engage employees is a topic for another book, but promoting authenticity, focusing on positive attributes, asking for critical feedback, and appreciating their value are excellent starting points.

Employees are most engaged when they feel a sense of empowerment and are placed in roles of influence and responsibility.

2. Digital capabilities. You'll need to implement holistic digital platforms and deliver a seamless experience. Customers increasingly choose to engage with brands across various digital channels that can deliver smarter, connected, personalized, and seamless experiences. This is a tough job, but creating engaging, multichannel, and personal experiences for your digital customers will deliver the best experience.

Disney's Seamless Success

Disney provides seamless digital experiences, right down to the smallest details. It starts with your initial experience on the entertainment giant's beautiful, mobile-responsive website. Once you've booked a trip, the My Disney Experience tool plans your entire trip, secures your Fast Pass, and even suggests where you should dine. In the park, you can use your mobile app to locate the attractions you want to visit, as well as view the estimated wait time for each of them. The Magic Band program acts as a hotel room key, Fast Pass, photo storage device, and a food ordering tool.

According to a study by Harvard Business Review Analytics Services, 87 per cent of polled executives said having the technology and infrastructure to study customer experience is crucial to making improvements. However, 75 per cent of the executives said their organizations lacked the technology for uniting systems that collect social, mobile, and e-commerce data to produce a single and directly accessible source of customer intelligence.

3. Cross-functional collaborations. As long as each business unit is an island by itself, there will be massive amounts of spent energy, financial leakage, and bad customer experiences. I call this bad experience "customer amnesia." It occurs because each time a customer interacts with a different unit or channel, the previous interaction is forgotten.

Brands have the most success when they focus on how people work together, know what their customers need, and understand the culture of the different units so a shared approach can be used to drive success.

You need to have a customer-centric mindset, where cross-functional collaboration serves as the gateway to untapped growth, innovation, and excellent service.

The Zappos Experiment

One company that is used as a benchmark for cross-functional collaborations is Zappos. In 2013, Zappos began experimenting with a controversial form of cross-functional collaboration called Holacracy. Holacracy is a method of decentralized management and organizational governance, in which authority and decision-making are distributed throughout self-organizing teams rather than being vested in management only.

Zappos employees are responsible for understanding how their role fits with the roles of others on the team. The teams are flexible, evolving according to the capabilities and the needs of team members. There is never a set job description, and multiple leaders emerge, depending on the current need.

While this style is not for everyone, no one can deny the superior customer experience that Zappos offers. The website is simple, intuitive, and easy to use; it's designed to make the buying and returning experience very enjoyable. According to Jon Wolske, a culture evangelist from Zappos Insights, 75 to 80 per cent of Zappos visitors are returning customers. Further, of the 25 per cent of customers who are new, about 40 per cent indicate that friends or family told them about the Zappos experience.

REPEATING THE PROCESS

Nurture Your Existing Customers So You Don't Get Dumped

Congrats are in order, but hold the applause.

You've spent all your time, effort, and money to define which customers you want to reach. New customers have even found you, and they like what you have to offer. They show your business love through word-of-mouth marketing and social media shout-outs to friends and family. The only problem is, most of you are still doing it wrong. Let me explain.

Many of you fall into the mindset of being comfortably numb. You think you've done what it takes and are reaping the rewards of success. You have empowered your employees to give the best customer service, and as a result, your customers just love you.

This is when many companies get a bit lazy. They feel content in their success and think there is only smooth sailing ahead. They are comfortably numb to the steps needed to maintain and grow their customer base.

Companies Need to Plug the Bathtub

Picture a bathtub. You want the tub to be filled with warm, delicious water, where you can soak your body and get that amazing feeling of relaxation.

Your company is the tub, and the water is the customer. The thing is, most companies are constantly focused on filling up the tub with fresh water (new customers) and don't understand why the tub is not getting full. The reason is that they forget to plug the bathtub from time to time and nurture their existing customers.

What on Earth Does This Mean?

The best analogy I can think of is being in a personal relationship. They say the grass is always greener on the other side, but I disagree. If you tend to your side, your grass, add passion, dedication, devotion, and love, then your grass is going to be the best there is. Or simply put, if you don't take care of the relationship and pay attention to your partner, over time, she may ask herself, *Why should I stay, because this, this, this, and that just aren't there anymore?* The spark has faded, and ultimately, your ignored partner will walk away. So don't be stupid, stupid. Don't give them a reason to walk away, and don't be the one to sing

> Don't it always seem to go
> That you don't know what you've got
> Till it's gone.

Don't give your customers a reason to try the grass on the other side. Nourish them so they don't move on to someone new in search of finding a brand that gives them the attention and love they desire.

A Question for Existing Customers

When was the last time you received an email from a brand that gave you a discount because you've been a loyal customer? When was the last time you, entirely out of the blue, were given a three-month extension to your gym membership because you've stayed with them for more than twelve months?

I'm assuming you can't think of the last time this happened to you. Businesses tend to offer the sweet deals to new customers as an incentive to buy their product or join their service. Businesses continually value fresh and new customers, while ignoring the existing, loyal customers.

Existing customers then get a bad taste in their mouth. They feel ignored, not important, and underappreciated. Many times, they leave and buy from another business or join another service that makes them feel important all over again. It seems so simple to appreciate our existing customers, yet we often don't.

However, when you nurture your customer relationships, you save money and expand profit margins. In fact, a report from Harvard

Business School stated that increasing customer retention rates by just 5 per cent can increase profits by 25 to 95 per cent.

How Do We Nurture Existing Customers?

You adapt or die. We are in the age of marketing Darwinism. It is the survival of the fittest, in a highly competitive, sophisticated digital world. This sets the stage for a new era of leadership, with new business models, charging behind a mantra of "adapt or die."

The best way to balance existing and new customers is by using the 80/20 rule. To nurture your existing customers, spend 80 per cent of your time and efforts on them. Find clever ways to show appreciation and gratitude by delighting them in ways that make them stay with you. Not because they have to, but because they want to. Make them part of your branding, product development, and marketing. Here are some simple ways to make them feel like they are part of your family:

Learn everything about them. Gathering data about your customer will drive decisions about future customer interactions. Study and analyse social media, email, and other data so you learn more about your customer. Data can also be segmented, so customers have an individualized experience. Segmentation ensures that you are nurturing your customers and their unique characteristics.

Send personalized, relevant emails. By sending customers personalized emails, you are demonstrating your brand's investment in their unique needs. If they've abandoned their shopping cart, you can send a friendly reminder. If they've been spending time on some particular product pages, you can follow up with more product information and benefits. Maybe it's been a year since they made their first online purchase. You can send them an email celebrating the anniversary and offering a discount.

Get social. Be proactive and reactive when it comes to managing your social media accounts. You can do this by responding to any queries or brand mentions as quickly as possible. Always add a personal touch along with your communications. Research shows that about 30 per cent of consumers prefer to deal with companies via social media rather than on the phone. Also, nearly half of social media users with annual incomes over $200k prefer social media interaction over live customer service. Getting social matters in today's digital age.

What about New Customers?

They are important too. Spend 20 per cent of your time and money on attracting new customers. With a powerful tribe of advocates on your side (existing customers), standing out from the crowd and earning customers' attention won't be much of a problem. It's a lot easier to be louder than the competition when it's the voice of your customers making all the noise for you.

So stop obsessing about targeting new customers by spending your time and money trying to get them to buy your product. In reality, it's a lot easier to sell to your existing customers. When you sell to an existing customer, you should get the same feeling and rewards you get when you sell to a new customer. Keeping your current customers happy and well looked after is critical to your long-term success.

You can't build a reputation on what you are going to do.

—Henry Ford

CHAPTER 6

HOW TO BUILD YOUR BRAND: BEHAVIOURS

Your Business's Success Is Built by Your Brand

Amazon CEO Jeff Bezos once said, "Your brand is what other people say about you when you're not in the room." No matter the size of your business, your customers are going to talk about you. Developing a good brand helps you take control of that discussion. But the concept of what a brand actually is has become increasingly convoluted, difficult to define, and hard to pin down with just one definition.

Defining a Brand

The trouble that many business leaders face with branding is that it's intangible, but it can have add many tangible benefits to your bottom line. Depending on what definition you follow, a brand could be anything from "the intangible sum of a product's attributes" (David Ogilvy) to "a person's perception of a product, service, experience, or organization" (*The Dictionary of Brand*). Some common themes do exist with all definitions: Branding is more than developing a logo. It's about the gut feeling that customers get when they see your product, service, or organization.

A Strong Brand Drives Your Business Forward

Defining your brand and understanding how it impacts your business is an important step. It guides your brand and leads your business forward. Identify what makes your brand unique, and uncover what makes your business unique as well. This allows you to build a marketing strategy that aligns with your brand. In doing so, you unlock your brand's full potential.

A strong brand isn't about your business's logo, products, or corporate colours. It goes beyond what your company looks like. Good branding increases the value of an organization. It provides direction and a sense of identity for your employees. Having a well-known brand can make attracting customers much easier.

Branding Is Often Neglected

Yet many small businesses and start-ups neglect their branding. They don't invest the necessary time and resources to develop their brand fully. Instead, they focus on delivering short-term, measurable financial results. The intangible results offered by branding simply don't stack up in the short term.

Because of this, small business owners view branding as a frivolous, tick-box-type activity. They believe that a logo, a range of products, an adequate website, some social media accounts, and a YouTube channel is enough to build their brand. But it isn't.

For everyday small business opportunities, this tactic can work. But if you want your business to scale, to expand globally, and to compete in a saturated market, then a strong brand is needed.

Branding: Just Do It

The iconic shoe brand Nike started out on the track fields in Washington. Founded by runner Phil Knight and coach Bill Bowerman, it was originally called Blue Ribbon Sports. A name, I think you'd agree, that would never catch on.

The Nike logo and "Just Do It" tagline are now recognized all over the world. But the Nike brand is built on more than just that. It sells a lifestyle. The only thing that's stopping you from becoming the next Apple or Nike is taking the time to develop a strong and clear brand vision, strategy, and tactics.

Creating a Strong Brand

There are a couple of things you should do to strengthen your brand:

Know your audience. To become the next Nike in your industry, you need to identify what drives your customers to purchase. Tap into their mindset, discover what they desire, and build your brand identity around that.

Mind the gap. Understand your brand gap (see below). This is the cognitive dissonance between your image and your profile. Knowing this allows you to bridge the gap with your branding.

Recognize who your business is and why your customers should care. What's your brand purpose? What makes your brand stand out, and what's your company story? Do you even have a story? There are many questions to ask yourself when building your brand.

Tell Your Brand's Story

Storytelling is vital to a good brand. This artform can make all the difference in setting a good brand apart from the best.

Gather round a bonfire. Stories have been told for millennia. People would gather around open fires to share great stories and pass them on to their children. A good story stands the test of time.

Create a movement. Define a common ground. Connect with your customers through storytelling. Create a common purpose or mission. The shoe brand TOMS was founded on the principle that for every pair of shoes sold, another pair would go to a child in need. It's now expanded to eyewear, coffee, and bags.

Lead a tribe. Customers are your best salespeople. When you foster passion in your customers, they'll follow you through thick and thin. It will also define your brand and exemplify what your company stands for. It's the ultimate way to bring your story, and brand, to life.

Of course, with leadership comes great responsibility. There's a ton of advice available on how to become a great leader. In short, make sure you present yourself in the best way possible. Focus on your strengths, your unique selling points, and your business's characteristics. Make sure you keep everything real and honest. Being false will turn people off your brand instantly.

The Many Benefits of Good Branding

There are many good reasons to build a brand. Don't be tempted to rush it. With so much at stake, it's important to think through your brand identity fully.

Having a strong brand will pay off in the long run. It makes your business more recognizable, fosters trust between your customers and company, and makes it easier to develop your product lines. Your branding will support your advertising, making it more cost-effective and giving you a greater return on your ad investment. It can increase your financial reach, inspire and drive your employees, and generate new customers.

If you want to get ahead of your competitors and guarantee long-term growth, build a strong brand. It's the foundation to everything else.

Knowing Your Audience Is Critical to Your Brand

A brand for a company is like a reputation for a person.
You earn reputation by trying to do hard things well.
—Jeff Bezos

What do Apple, Chanel, and Nike all have in common? They know their audience. Identifying your audience is the first step in building a strong brand, as these successful companies have proven. Each of them targets different customers, with differing needs and desires. By uncovering these drives, Apple, Chanel, and Nike have built brands that resonate with their customers.

Know Their Desires

Your customers will make or break your business. In order to create a company image and marketing that connects with your customers, you need to understand who they are. You need to uncover how they think, determine what they want, and understand their lingo. Figure this out, and you'll be able to match their expectations and desires.

No People = No Brand

According to brand master Marty Neumeier, a brand is defined by a person's gut feeling about a product, service, or organization. People should be at the heart of your brand. Without them, you don't have a brand. You simply have a shell of an idea.

At its most basic level, your target audience is comprised of

- people or businesses who directly need or want your product,
- those who influence the people who need or want your product, and
- your supporters and brand ambassadors.

In other words, the people who pay you directly, the people who convince others to pay you, and your support system.

Identify Your Audience

There are several ways to identify your different audiences. In really simple terms, you have to look at their needs and wants. First, find people who really want your product.

Now, the reasons why they might want your product are varied. Price is one of those factors. Depending on your price, your product or service might be considered a commodity, a need, or a luxury. If you get your messaging right, then you can charge a premium for your product, and it'll become something your customers really desire. If that's the strategy you want to go for, of course. Chanel follows this tactic by pricing its goods high and using luxury materials like lambskin that are designed to last a long time. On the other end of the market, retailer Primark capitalizes on fast fashion and rock-bottom prices.

This says something about the type of audience you should be targeting. If you want to set a high price point for your goods, then you should confirm that it's within your audience's budget. If it will take them a while to save up to purchase, you need to give them a good reason why they should do that. That could be in terms of superior quality, exclusivity, longevity, or as a status symbol.

Don't Overlook Customers

It's also important to identify your target audience, as you might be overlooking a group of customers who are perfect for your business. Knowing the different groups of people who use your business allows you to determine their fit and value. Prioritizing certain groups in your marketing prevents you from wasting resources on people who won't purchase or targeting an audience that's too broad.

Communicate Company-Wide

Once you've identified your target audience, you should communicate this across your business. Everyone in your company needs to know who your audience is. Your employees are the main ambassadors for your brand. They need to feel empowered and able to speak to your audience.

Be Accurate

Having the right audience identified, but with the wrong analysis about their needs, is worse than having no target audience. Your information about their needs and wants must be accurate; otherwise, your communication and offering won't match up to what they want. There'll be a gap between what they want and what you believe they want.

Get Specific

You can't sell to everyone. Nike doesn't try to sell to people who don't like sportswear. Your products and services won't be for everyone. Therefore, try to get as specific as you can when defining your audience. A retailer that specializes in running shoes might define their target audience as "fashion-conscious people aged 21-35 who run at least once a week."

Create Emotion

Remember, when creating a brand, you want to evoke emotion in your customers. To do this, you need to really drill down into the specific desires and needs of your customers. Ideally, you'd do this one-on-one with target audience members. At the very least, you should be considering the following:

Their demographics: the age, gender, race, education, and occupation of your customer.

Their geographical location: including whether they usually shop in-store or online. Looking at the type of area (city vs countryside) where they live and work can also be insightful.

Their psychographics: this includes the thought processes people go through when deciding on a purchase or interacting with a brand. Their desires and needs fall under this as well.

There's several ways to obtain this information. Interviewing people who fit your ideal customer profile is best. However, if pushed for time and resources, you can also consider focus groups, secondary market research, software like Google Analytics, and social media listening.

Employees Must Commit

Your brand is more than just your logo and imagery. Everything, from your messaging to your customer service needs to remain consistent. People need to know exactly what to expect when they interact with your brand. Apple isn't just known for cutting-edge technology. The Apple Geniuses in every store also add to the brand experience.

Don't forget that a good brand will connect with people on an emotional level. You've likely seen the emotion invoked in people who queue for days to buy new Apple iPhones. People want to feel good when they purchase a brand. Most products aren't physically worth their selling price. Apple iPhones cost around $200 to make. However, at launch, they retail for around $500 to $700, depending on the model and specs. The value of an iPhone far exceeds its physical worth. That's largely down to branding. Apple has found the perfect formula for its brand: understanding its audience, creating a brand that resonates with them, and having employees commit to the brand.

Consistency Is Key

People like to do business with companies that they recognize. By developing a brand they know, that aligns with their values, you make it more likely that they will choose your business over competitors. Make sure your branding is consistent and easy to recognize so you can capitalize on this opportunity.

Be Unforgettable

Making your brand well-known and memorable also increases the likelihood that people will tell others about you. We all recommend brands to our friends and family. If someone cannot remember a brand, then they're probably not going to mention it to others.

People Come First

Get your brand right, and people will continue to use your business for years to come. Get it wrong, and you'll waste countless resources on the wrong marketing and audience. When developing your brand, you must uncover your audience's mindset. Everything leads from there.

Your brand is the reason why someone will choose you over a competitor, why a customer will return, and why people will pay much more for your products. To build a strong brand, you need to put people first.

MIND THE GAP

Bridging the Brand Gap

Today's consumers shop differently. They don't buy products based simply on features or services or because of what can be offered. Many make their purchasing decisions based on brands they feel they can trust. Have you ever been to a foreign country and automatically navigated towards the familiarity of a Starbucks or McDonald's? It's because you know what to expect from those companies. That's the power of branding.

A good brand is worth a lot of money to an organization. Starbucks' brand value is currently estimated at $47 billion. McDonald's, the most valuable fast food brand in the world, is a whopping $129 billion. It should be every company's goal to move from having customers see you as a business to having them see you as a brand.

But a good brand can always fail because of the brand gap.

Introducing the Brand Gap

Brands are now the net sum of lots of different interactions that create a feeling of trust (or distrust) in consumers. From billboards to TV ads, from social media to sponsorship deals, they all add up to a gut feeling in your customers. To achieve a strong brand, you need a new approach to marketing.

That's where the brand gap comes in. It's the gap between your marketing team's strategy and creativity. In most companies, there is a gulf that has appeared between right-brain-oriented marketers and left-brain creatives. Here, one group isn't aware of what the other is doing, and vice versa. There is constant tension between the two camps. The left-brainers are analytical, logical, and verbal. Meanwhile, the right-brainers are emotional, visual, and intuitive. When communication and understanding breaks down between the two, you get a brand gap.

That means that your strategy doesn't get translated into a creative initiative in the way that you intended. If your brand gap is too great, your strategy will fail completely.

Consequences of a Brand Gap

A company suffering from a brand gap cannot effectively communicate who it is to its customers. That means it cannot build a strong relationship with consumers; they don't know what to expect when interacting with the company. That undermines its position and strength in the market. In turn, this offers opportunities for competitors to take the company's place as a brand leader.

It's a serious problem, and it starts when you fail to bring your right- and left-brained team together.

Marketing Is More Complex

Of course, creative marketers do still exist. However, they are becoming far fewer in number. Marketing itself is becoming more complex. It requires right-brain, logical thinkers who can work with numbers and many different marketing channels. There's a lot more analytics in marketing nowadays, and that's doing away with a lot of creatives.

But with audience's attention spans at a premium, we need differentiation and innovation now more than ever. When brands connect emotionally with customers, their business stands out amongst the crowd. In short, we need to bridge the brand gap.

So how do we achieve this?

How to Remove the Gap

A brand, and marketing as a function, is about facilitating the sales process. It needs to communicate value and entice consumers to a brand. You need to begin here, with this understanding, in order to drive your creative process.

Your brand and any designs need to win attention and create interest.

You must also understand that you cannot completely control or perfect a brand. It's something that can be refined over time, but it'll always evolve with changing needs and culture. Instead of focussing on perfecting it, work on making your brand consistent across all your marketing channels. That's how you develop that instinctive gut feeling in your customers.

Your brand must be charismatic. Think of companies like Apple and Coca-Cola. They've positioned themselves as exciting, innovative, joy-inducing brands. Anyone who has seen the queues at an iPhone launch can vouch for the happiness that Apple induces in their customers. Coca-Cola's tagline used to be "Open Happiness."

Creating this kind of aspirational brand builds a strong relationship with your customers.

Building an Aspirational Brand

There are several areas you need to consider when bridging your brand gap and creating an aspirational brand:

Differentiate. We stand up and pay attention when something different crosses our path. We notice the unexpected. It's something your brand can use to gain a competitive advantage. Smoothie brand Innocent takes part in the Big Knit every winter. This doesn't just give it charity brownie points. It also makes its smoothies stand out on every shop shelf. Every winter, its bottles wear their own miniature woolly hats. Each unique bottle draws the consumer's eyes to the brand.

A key part of being differentiated is to remain focused. You must understand what your brand is, why it is appealing, and what makes it different. Don't be scared of narrowing your audience and shrinking down your niche. It won't cut you off from potential opportunities. In fact, being focused is the only way to be truly competitive.

Collaborate. A brand cannot develop in isolation. It requires all sorts of different people with a range of skills and specialties to come together. That includes right and left-brained people.

Innovate. You must appeal to your customers' emotions, and that means you cannot do what every other company in your industry is doing. You must innovate. When every competitor zags, make sure you zig.

Validate. This is how you ensure that your brand resonates with the real world and not just inside your company. You might think that your brand is the bee's knees, but you need to confirm this by doing a concept test with at least ten people from outside your company. You can also do a swap test (like swapping your logo or name with a competing brand) to test different elements of your brand. If your results are better than or equal to the competitor, then your brand needs more work.

Cultivate. All brands are living things. They must change with the times. Make sure you have processes that allow you to monitor and understand the outside world, and then apply that expertise to your brand and internal culture. This is what keeps your brand authentic and builds a stronger gut feeling with your audience.

Mind the Gap

The brand gap is a risk for every business. Logic and creativity can coexist; they just need to be on the same page. That requires several types of discipline. Five, to be exact: differentiation, collaboration, innovation, validation, and cultivation.

Make sure your teams are united under these five disciplines, and you'll have no trouble creating a charismatic and strong brand.

WHO ARE YOU? WHY SHOULD I CARE?

Your Brand Needs a Purpose

> When you find your WHY, you don't hit snooze
> no more! You find a way to make it happen!
> —Eric Thomas

Scottish author William Barclay once said there were two great days in someone's life: the day they were born and the day they discovered why. Your brand is exactly the same.

Your purpose is why you get up in the morning. It's why you commute to work, why you go throughout your day, go to sleep, and then do it all over again. Many people don't have a clear purpose. That means they return home from work feeling unfulfilled.

Purpose drives action. Dr. Martin Luther King Jr. gave the American people a purpose in 1963 when he described his dream of racial equality. Leadership can be extremely powerful in generating a purpose. In your business, purpose trickles down from the top.

Why Brands Need Purpose

Giving your brand a purpose doesn't just affect your employees. It can also motivate your customers into feeling like they are making a change or having an impact on the world.

Consider this question: who are you and why should I care? If you were asked that out on the street, you might think it odd or downright rude. But it defines the kind of company you have or want to have.

Consumers are bombarded with ten thousand brand messages every day. Attention spans are at a premium. People need to decide which brands to pay attention to and what to ignore. Brands with a clear purpose, one that aligns with their values, are more likely to be noticed. Eight in ten consumers say they feel more loyal to brands with a purpose.

Apple has the motto "Think Different." It perfectly describes the brand's "why": "With everything we do, we aim to challenge the status quo. We aim to think different." How does it achieve this? With beautifully designed, user-friendly products, enthusiastic employees, and modern stores.

Purpose = Profits

Having a purpose pays off profit-wise as well. Research has found that companies with a clear purpose have growth rates 10 per cent higher than companies without a purpose. The same report discovered that 42 per cent of businesses without a purpose had a revenue drop. In the same time period, 85 per cent of purpose-led companies showed positive revenue growth.

The *Financial Times* reported that companies with a purpose that extended beyond making money, ended up with shareholder returns that were six times higher than profit-driven competitors.

What Purpose Is Not

There's sometimes a mix-up between purpose and corporate social responsibility (CSR). Whilst CSR projects are influenced by purpose, they are not one and the same. Brand purpose encompasses so much more.

Another thing to be aware of is that your purpose needs to stay current, which means it's not to be set in stone or absolute. In fact, the most effective ones change with the times. Your brand purpose can evolve and adapt to the changing needs of society.

Brands don't always have to change the biggest problems in the world. Whilst some brands seek social justice or fight climate change and inequality, many others can solve problems in the everyday. Pret works with local food banks and homeless charities to distribute its unsold food, for example.

Remember, your brand cannot please everyone. Your purpose won't always achieve worldwide happiness, but it should inform everything that your business does at every single point of the customer journey.

What Purpose Is

The brand purpose is the business's ultimate reason for being, the reason why it exists, beyond making money. It could be the very reason the brand was founded, like how shoe brand TOMS provides shoes and other products for people in need.

Having a purpose gives your brand a relevance in society, hopefully one that will give it longevity. It helps your employees unite under a common cause. It should be the foundation to all your business decisions. It's the guiding force of your business.

A great purpose is woven into the fabric of your business. It's in your product development, your customer experience, your marketing, and everything in between.

Under Armour's brand purpose is to "Empower Athletes Everywhere." It goes on to say that athletes come in all shapes and sizes. It supports the underdog. Under Armour wants to break the mould, and this shines through in its designs, marketing, and sponsorship deals.

In doing so, it creates online and offline experiences that are memorable to its audience. It adds value to consumers' lives and builds the kind of loyalty that you cannot get through a commercial or billboard.

Debunking Some Terms

Up until now, we've been discussing brand purpose. When researching yours, you might also come across the terms *vision* and *mission*. Let me explain the difference between these terms:

- **Purpose** is why your brand exists. It's the big reason for being, and it's more than just making profits or driving shareholder value.
- **Vision** is where you want to get to. It's where you want your business to be in the future.
- **Mission** is what you need to do to achieve your vision. It can be specific initiatives or tactics centred around your marketing, product development, and operations.

One final aspect is your brand's values. This is how your organization needs to behave in order to achieve your mission and vision. These are qualities and behaviours that your organization prizes above all. Apple's core value is innovation, whilst Under Armour's is equality and loving athletes, and finally Google's "Don't be evil" is a statement all by itself.

Unlocking all these things builds the foundation on which to build everything else.

How to Do This

So how can you bring your brand purpose to life? First, it must be part of your company culture. Your employees need to know about your purpose, to believe in it, and to live your brand purpose every single day. Culture is the first product of any business.

Your purpose can have a dedicated CSR initiative or fancy marketing campaign, like Ariel's "Share the Load" campaign. But it is much more than that. Think of when you walk into an Apple store. It's shiny and well-lit. It screams innovation and modernity. Apple Geniuses embody the brand purpose and have become as well known as iPhones and Macs.

It's important to measure any purpose-driven campaigns. Not just on the usual marketing and vanity metrics, but on their impact. For Ariel's "Share the Load" campaign, a good metric to track would be how many men began to do housework in family homes in the months following the campaign launch. Your metrics must help you understand how well your purpose has achieved your higher objectives.

The Purpose-Driven Era

We are in a new era, where purpose-driven brands are outpacing all the rest. Purpose is critical to your brand. People are more attracted to brands with purpose, both as consumers and potential employees. With a purpose, your brand can make a profit and change the world. Embrace your purpose, and you'll find a deeper level of meaningfulness in your work.

We All Have a Story; What Is Yours?

> Story, as it turns out, was crucial to our evolution,
> more so than opposable thumbs. Opposable thumbs
> let us hang on; story told us what to hang on to.
>
> —Lisa Cron

Bonfire Marketing

Have you ever tried to light a bonfire? There is an art to it. You need to have the right amount of wood and kindling, and you have to keep it lit once it's going. A well-lit bonfire can keep your tribe warm for many hours.

The same applies to your marketing. More specifically, to the stories you communicate with your audience.

Since the Start

Bonfires have been around for more than four hundred thousand years. Tribes would gather around bonfires to listen to storytellers and watch performers. In this way, human history, along with tales, myths, and life lessons, were passed from parent to child, person to person, until the current day.

Gather Your Tribe

Think of your customers as your tribe. Gather them around your bonfire, and use it to inform, entertain, and enlighten them. That sounds pretty easy, right? Well, if the stories you tell your tribe don't hit the right note, then your tribe may leave for another bonfire. If you don't maintain your bonfire, your stories will go cold, and conversations will fade.

Influencers Are Tribal

Many businesses struggle to keep their bonfires lit. Large brands and small businesses alike wish to use channels like social media to sell their products and services. It's rare to find companies that do this well. Except for one group: the online entrepreneurs, the influencers. Many influencers don't intend to start a business, at least in the beginning. They have a passion for health, beauty, cooking, fitness, and so forth. This leads them to create content around this passion, attracting fellow-minded people and building a community. From this, a business surfaces, and sales will come naturally. There are many companies that are breaking the mould in this way. Sweat with Kayla is a fitness-focused one, and Deliciously Ella is another.

The majority of brands have the opposite origin story. They created a product and then used social media and other channels to encourage people to buy it. Their messaging often focuses on the product and not the passion behind it. Social selling, therefore, is much harder for them. The only way these businesses can gain the kind of engagement that influencers enjoy is to create a tribe.

Adidas has created a running community. It also uses influencers to help promote its brand and to gain the interest of their followers. Take a look at its Instagram, and you'll see partnerships with musicians, fitness influencers, and other celebrities.

Build Your Tribe

So what makes a good tribe?

- It needs to be united towards a common ideal or goal.
- It's under one leader.
- A tribe needs a shared interest.
- It also needs a way to communicate.

Communication between your tribe members is often overlooked. Give them a place to talk to each other. That could be a Facebook group or another online community page. People want to find others they relate to. Facilitate this, and your brand will benefit as a result.

Journalist and advertising strategist Matthew Bryan Beck discussed the rise of digital tribalism. We're naturally inclined to group together. Social media has given us access to whole new groups of people to connect with. Smartphones have led consumers to be online all the time. There are now mobile villages, where people hang out based on their shared interests. Businesses need to find these tribes and take advantage of them, or create their own.

Research Your Tribe

To understand what interests your tribe and where they like to hang out, you need to research them thoroughly. Check out where they spend their time, what they spend their time on, what they need, and what they desire. From this, you can identify the people who are likely to be most interested in your story. People ignore stories that don't interest them, so don't waste your time and resources talking to people who won't stay around your bonfire.

Make sure your story and passion are genuine. Customers can sense a fake story a mile away. Around a bonfire, you're held much more accountable. In 2018, influencer Elle Darby got into hot water with the media and her followers for trying to swap a hotel stay for a review and social media posts.

How to Tell Great Stories

Without good stories, your tribe isn't going to stick around. Use empathy, personalization, and memorability to make your stories interesting:

Empathy. This involves telling a story that interests people and that lets them imagine that they are a part of it. Think of what interests your target audience, not what you want to sell or tell them. Sweat with Kayla does this well. The BBG community makes everyone a part of the Kayla fitness journey.

Personalization. People don't just connect to a good story. If it relates to them in some way, they will remember it and tell it to others. Make your customers the heroes of the stories you tell them, and your products will sell themselves. One Drinks highlights a good example of this in action. For every drink bought, customers are providing water for people in need.

Memorability. What is remarkable about your story? How can you make people remember your brand? It doesn't have to be fancy or expensive. Simply getting people involved online can make them remember your message. Doritos ran the highly successful "Crash the Super Bowl" campaign that allowed consumers to create their own Super Bowl ads. It's helped to grow Doritos from a $1.54 billion brand in 2006 to currently $16 billion.

Light Your Bonfire

Bonfire marketing isn't about pushing products. It is about creating a community of people who are informed, enlightened, and entertained by your brand and their fellow community members. As Seth Godin once said, "Leadership is the art of giving people a platform for spreading ideas that work."

Anything could happen around your bonfire. The next big thing could be created within your community. Importantly, your brand will benefit by association.

To keep your bonfire going, make sure you always show up. Give people a place to share their ideas. Communicate with a consistent voice, and share your passions and beliefs. This way, your bonfire will light up your brand for a lifetime.

STORYTELLING

Your Brand Needs to Tell Good Stories

Imagine that you're meeting someone new, at an event or a dinner party. You'd ask questions to get to know them better, right? When we meet someone new, we want to know about their lives, their views, and their beliefs, and look to find similarities with our own. The same applies to your brand. To really make your brand memorable, you need to make it tell a story.

We've been conditioned to tell and listen to stories since our earliest days. The bedtime story is a ritual in many family homes. That doesn't change as we get older, although we may move away from books as our main source of stories to comics and movies.

Stories around a Campfire

Even cavemen were keen on a good story. The oldest form of storytelling is said to lie deep in some caves in France. The Chauvet Cave paintings depict different animals, including bears, horses, bison, and lions. The true meaning of these paintings are now lost to us, but they do highlight that we have been telling stories for a very long time.

Our ancestors also used to gather around fires to tell stories. Not much has changed. Richard Branson, founder of the Virgin Group, enjoys gathering his team around a fire to tell stories. He says, "Storytelling is the best way we have of coming up with new ideas."

Stories Connect to Customers

As a brand, you want to connect with your customers. Telling your story is a key part of this. With a well-told story, you can shape how people see your brand. Similar to how you connect with others through common experiences and values, customers connect more with a brand they can relate to. People buy from businesses they like. If they enjoy the stories you share, they'll return, time and time again.

Apple is a brand that's nailed storytelling. Watch any Apple product reveal, and you'll see storytelling in action. In 2018, a keynote showcased the company's developers and the hard work they put into creating Apple's features and apps. The story told is one of dedication and missed family dinners. It makes you buy into Apple's products, not just as an amazing piece of technology, but as labours of love.

"Great brands and great businesses have to be great storytellers," Apple Store Chief Angela Ahrendts once said. "We have to tell authentic, emotive, and compelling stories because we're building relationships with people and every great relationship has to be built on trust."

Employees Benefit Too

This doesn't just motivate customers to purchase products. It encourages employees to do more, to raise their game. Great storytelling results in improved employee engagement, better customer service, better retention, and increased profits.

Marketing Failures

Many marketers believe they're already good storytellers. But simply having a content plan in place doesn't mean you tell good stories. At its core, storytelling isn't about what we do. It's about who we are.

When a marketing campaign neglects storytelling, it shows in the lack of customer engagement and how people respond to it. Think of all those billboards out there with "BUY ONE, GET ONE FREE" emblazoned across them as a way to get attention. Yes, customers might visit once to get the offer. But to keep them coming back consistently, you need to tell them your story and have them relate to it.

According to the Content Marketing Institute, 65 per cent of organizations are still in the early stages of implementing a content marketing strategy. In over half, there's only one content marketer to serve the entire organization. Only 38 per cent of UK marketers say they have a documented content marketing strategy.

In all of these cases, for various reasons, marketers don't understand who they are trying to reach, what's important to those people, or why they will interact with a brand's content. That's why (according to LinkedIn) 95 per cent of content fails to connect with its audience. Sadly now, it seems, content is created to go viral instead of being of value to a customer.

So how do you create good stories that resonate with audiences?

Think back to a time when a story really grabbed your attention. What made it good? It probably contained some element that you could relate to. By making stories relevant, you can get people's attention and hold it. Make those stories informative, and they're more likely to be shared across people's networks. Instead of aiming for virality, therefore, you should be making stories relevant and useful.

Relevance. Relevant stories need to talk about the everyday successes, concerns, and challenges of your customers. Think about their desires, their needs, and their wants. Think about their values and what issues they focus on. Then consider how your brand can become the hero in their story. For example, Airbnb highlights hosts in different countries and provides travel inspiration through its dedicated magazine.

Usefulness. Make sure your content is useful for your audience. Again, knowing particular pain points and concerns can help you with this. Nike provides inspiration, running clubs, music, and tips through the Nike+ running app.

The goal of your stories is to communicate with your people and to build a community. Importantly, this community needs to feel empowered by your content and to feel like it has made a difference in their lives.

Stories Must Be Real

However, your stories must be authentic. Consumers can smell a fake story a mile away. PepsiCo was caught out by misleading customers into believing that its Naked Juices were healthier than they actually were. It had to change the labels on some juices, like its Kale Blazer drink that contained more orange juice than kale.

Shift to Stories

Marketers need to make a shift from prioritizing content to creating stories. It's storytelling that will differentiate your brand. Good stories are engaging, relevant, useful, believable, and aspirational. They have the power to transform the way we see the world, which is a noble cause for any brand.

Good storytelling is a delicate balance of evoking the right emotion, creating human connections, and understanding the motivations of your audience. Getting it right can be a challenge for businesses, but it's worth doing, because stories bring meaning to your brand.

The Science of Storytelling

Everyone loves stories. A good story has the power to compel others, to inspire people, even to shape the world. They can comfort, connect, transform, and even heal. Everyone has a story to tell, but not everyone can tell it well. There is a science to it, though, a formula you can learn. Through this, you can develop your own method to tell your story.

Famous author Rudyard Kipling once said, "I keep six honest serving men (they taught me all I knew), their names are what and why and when and how and where and who."

Even this great master of storytelling understood that all stories have a basic structure and answer fundamental questions about the who, the what, the when, and so forth. The facts of a story matter. However, buried beneath those facts is the true key to storytelling. It's building an emotional connection with the reader.

Postcard Stories

Take a look at whiskey brand Jack Daniels. All over the London Underground, you can see its "Postcards from Lynchburg" campaign. Each postcard tells the story of the maker of Jack Daniels and the small town where it originates. It adds depth to the brand and draws the reader in. How? Through emotive language and vivid description. You can almost read it with a Southern drawl.

Then there's TED Talks. Ever seen one? You might think there's magic in the air when the speaker talks, but it's just great storytelling in action. The speaker relays a story, captures the audience's imagination, and explains the lessons learnt from that story.

The Listener

But let's consider the other side of the story. Because a key part of any story is the listener. After all, you need to know your audience to understand how to speak to them. Poet Ralph Waldo Emerson once observed that people are always telling you what they really think (whether they know it or not).

We're always broadcasting our inner thoughts. They are revealed through our attitude, our point of view, whenever we volunteer it in an offhand manner. This is why you need to master the art of storytelling, to develop the discipline of knowing what to say and what not to.

The Science

The science behind great stories is really quite simple. Ever been stuck watching a boring PowerPoint presentation? When that happens, two parts of your brain are activated: Broca's area and Wernicke's area. Those are the parts that decode words into meaning. That's it, nothing else.

Listen to a story, and it's a different matter. When someone tells a story, our brains light up with the activity and experiences mentioned in the tale. If the story contains a steaming bowl of tomato soup, our sensory cortex gets activated. If the protagonist of the story is running through twisted alleyways, our motion cortex springs to life.

Furthermore, the brains of the storyteller and the listener actually sync up during these moments. You can make people feel exactly what you're experiencing. That's incredibly powerful for a brand.

Ads which invoke an emotional response in consumers have been found to have a far greater influence on their intent to buy. TV ads that provoke emotion are three times as effective, and print ads are twice as effective. In fact, the likeability of an ad is the most predictive measure of increasing sales.

The Structure of a Story

Now let's look at the ideal structure of a good story. All stories need to have a clear beginning, middle, and an end. You cannot tell an effective story unless you know where to start, where you plan to end up, and the journey along the way. Without a clear structure, you risk meandering and wasting your audience's time and attention span.

Here are ten principles behind storytelling. They're based on the brilliant advice of Bobette Buster, a story consultant, lecturer, and screenwriter. She works with some of the major studios including Pixar, Disney, and Sony Animation (to name a few).

1. **Speak to me as a friend.** Keep your language simple and on your audience's level.
2. **Remember context.** Don't forget to explain the time, place, and surroundings. Describe, don't comment on the scene. Try to use sensory descriptions so listeners can picture themselves there.

3. **Use active verbs.** Action is key, or more simply put, how would Hemingway say it?

4. **Mix it up.** Take two contrasting ideas, images, or thoughts, and mix them together. This will grab your audience's attention from the get-go.

5. **Detail.** What's the one thing that captures the essence of your story? Remember, brains sync up when a story is told. So don't be shy with the details of what you're feeling and experiencing.

6. **The spark.** Reflect on the idea or experience that originally captivated you, and hand it over to your audience. Let them carry the flame.

7. **Be vulnerable.** Don't be scared to show emotion. Invite your audience to experience your doubt, confusion, sorrow, anger, joy, and delight.

8. **Use your senses.** Because your audience's brains will respond to your sensory information, make sure you use all your senses. It will create a deeper connection with the listener.

9. **Be yourself.** Authenticity is key. A story is as much about you as it is anything else.

10. **Let go.** Let your story build to its natural punchline, and then end it. Leave your audience wanting more.

Where appropriate, you can use statistics and other information to build the credibility of your story. Format your story to its appropriate channel, whether that's a vlog, blog, Tweet, or Instagram post. Also, get people involved in your story. User-generated content can be a powerful way of spreading your story's message once it has been told.

Storytelling has been around since our caveman days. It is native to all of us. You just have to do it. Dare to be personal, to open yourself up and be vulnerable, and to listen to others' stories as well.

MOVEMENT

Introducing Movement Marketing

Can you catch lightning in a bottle? Practically speaking, it might be a little hard to contain within those brittle glass walls. But that's exactly what movement marketing is. It's the moment when a brand (including the values and products that it represents) becomes more than just something people buy. In a way, the message behind the brand becomes bigger than the brand itself. That's powerful stuff.

By creating a movement, you begin something that unites people and becomes part of their lives. It's difficult to master. True brand-fuelled movements are as rare as unicorns and hard to deconstruct. But if you get it right, you'll have a long-term marketing strategy that won't just place your brand at the forefront of your industry; it might even change the world.

What's Movement Marketing?

Let's step back for a second and look at what movement marketing is. Broadly speaking, it's a brand-fuelled movement that creates an enduring phenomenon which organically transcends the brand. It connects and engages customers with each other, the brand, and the bigger movement itself.

In an increasingly competitive, noisy, and cluttered marketplace, movements can help build communities and mobilize people. Lauder Professor at the Wharton School of Business, Jerry Wind, and Wharton Future of Advertising Program Executive Director, Catherine Hays, put it well when they said, "All movements, regardless of their genesis, address an unmet need, galvanize people, and truly let the people take it over."

That means that a brand itself cannot be a movement, but it can help spawn one. Usually this occurs when a brand meets a social trend, an unmet need, or an untapped passion.

Movements at Work

TOMS achieves this well. It was founded on the basis that for every pair of shoes it sold, it would give another pair to someone in need. It has since expanded to providing glasses and water to developing countries, plus investment and social entrepreneurship projects. Although the concept and mission were close to founder Blake Mycoskie's heart, it was the brand's customers who sparked the movement.

Then you have WeWork. Their mission is to build a community where people work to build a life, not just for a living. It's at the forefront of a wider mission where people prioritize personal fulfilment over the traditional career ladder or earning money.

Characteristics

Generally speaking, there are five characteristics that are essential for strong brands. Only strong brands can spur a movement.

Create emotion. All successful brands inspire and evoke emotion, but a movement occurs when a company or brand makes a grand statement, and its customers get behind it.

Encourage involvement. Great movements will offer opportunities for customers and employees to become involved and empowered. There needs to be a common meeting place for everyone to communicate and inspire each other.

Build communities. Brands can achieve this through social media (such as Facebook groups) or in real life. WeWork has a physical community established in every office and holds regular events. It also has a virtual one via a Slack group.

Commitment. If people feel they are part of a movement, they will commit to it in the long term.

Authenticity. People can smell a fake a mile away. Only authentic brands will succeed in creating a movement. The movement itself needs to be part of a brand's bottom line, and a certain amount of accountability means stakeholders will be invested in it.

Key Barriers

There are some key barriers to achieving great movement marketing. You cannot create a movement if you're only focused on your return on investment (ROI). If your organization has silos that prevent people working together effectively, then your movement will likely fail. Therefore, slow-moving, inflexible, and overly bureaucratic companies aren't going to make movements. Movement marketing cannot be reversed engineered, either. A successful brand-fuelled movement cannot be retrofitted to a brand's DNA. Instead, it needs to be the other way around: a mission with a company built from it, like TOMS.

Beyond the Normal

When a brand-fuelled movement moves beyond a normal brand, the following things happen:

- It contributes to the greater good or to some purpose within broader society.

- It captures something of the moment. Both 2016 presidential campaigns tapped into the deeper cultural and political attitudes of the time and ultimately created movements that were bigger than their candidates and platforms.

- There is a strong call to action and a clear role for a brand's customers to play.

- It drives cultural or behavioural change, aligned with a fundamental shift in social values; for example, WeWork and the movement towards working as a lifestyle.

- It has an enduring impact; if you can make a documentary about the brand, it's a movement.

Positive Impacts

This is illustrated perfectly by Small Business Saturday. American Express founded Small Business Saturday to support local companies. It meets all the criteria for a movement. There's a purpose and a strong emotional component. The call to action is built on local values, personal connections, and community support. It asks people to shop local, on the first Saturday following Thanksgiving. It has grown quickly since beginning in 2010. Small Business Saturday is now held across all fifty US states and has had a shout-out from the president. Last year, almost half of all Americans shopped locally on Small Business Saturday.

There's also ongoing support for small business owners all year round from American Express, helping them build on the momentum from Small Business Saturday. 90 per cent of consumers state that the movement has had a positive impact on their local community.

Unique to You

Of course, all movements are unique. There's no playbook for making a movement. Plus, some brands might not wish to create a movement; resources might be seen as better invested elsewhere. However, many companies would pay top dollar for the kind of rapport that movement marketing can create.

All businesses want a warm, authentic, and long-lasting emotional connection with customers. It forms the foundation of any strong brand. In that way, movement marketing can create something beyond a brand that sweeps a company along with it. As a movement grows, so too can a business. There are untapped opportunities for brands to capitalize on social trends and help make a better world. You just have to be aware of what's out there and how your business can help. With the right steps, your brand can be at the centre of a movement that changes the world.

TRIBES

How to Maximize Your Tribe

Consider many great brands today. Across all industries, the one thing they have in common is loyal customers. After all, you cannot grow your business if you don't retain your customers. Keep your customers happy, and they'll keep returning. Plus, they'll bring their friends.

Passionate People Talk

People like talking about the stuff that they love. If they enjoy your products, then they will talk about you to their friends. It's something that happens naturally. Don't try to force it. Focus on providing good quality products and excellent service. Your customers will begin to do the rest.

McKinsey discovered that word of mouth can generate more than twice the sales of paid advertising. In other words, people much prefer to hear about new stuff from their peers than from a billboard.

Cut the Noise

Considering that we're bombarded with ten thousand marketing messages a day, it's little wonder that marketing isn't as effective at converting people. In an increasingly crowded marketplace, brands must work hard to stand out. Conventional marketing will only take you so far and can be time and resource heavy.

Instead, you need a community of supporters to speak for you. That's why influencer marketing has really taken off.

But you don't have to hire a pricey influencer to achieve the same sales. Many loyal customers would be happy to promote your brand. You just have to inspire them to do so. That means turning them into advocates.

Advocacy and Loyalty

Often, the terms *brand loyalists* and *brand advocates* get confused. They aren't the same. Loyalists are customers who return time and time again. But they might not tell their network about you.

However, brand advocates are loyal customers who proactively share stuff about you. The key here is that they are proactive. You don't have to encourage them to tell people about you because they are already invested in the success of your brand. These people are invaluable to your business.

Employees Count Too

Your customers aren't your only source of advocates. Employees can make some of your best brand advocates. More than half of consumers see employees as trusted sources of information about a brand. Your employees are often the first experience someone has with your brand, so it makes sense to cultivate them as advocates. This is a strategy that Apple has employed very well. Walk into any store, and you'll see the passion for Apple products written on every employee's face. The excitement is palpable at new product launches, and a lot of that emotion comes from its workforce.

Encouraging Advocacy

You cannot encourage someone to become an advocate using the same strategy you use to sell your products. You need to give people a good reason to talk about you.

There's several things you need to keep in mind when doing this:

1. **Stay focused.** Don't be tempted to be all things to everyone. You'll just lose your unique message and purpose. Instead, focus on doing one thing well for a clearly defined audience. By doing this, you help people recognize your brand as a go-to for a

specific niche. Ikea is known for selling flat-pack furniture. It's simple, reasonably priced, and ideal for urban living. Ikea's target market is people who need good quality furniture at a reasonable price, that they can fit in the car and assemble in their apartment.

2. **Tell stories.** Every brand has a story. You might not think yourself the next Mark Twain, but you can certainly tell a compelling tale. Just make sure it's relevant to your audience and unique to your brand.

3. **Be real.** People resonate with real brands. Don't be afraid to show your true colours. Equally, don't try to fake it. People can sense a dupe a mile away. If you're found to be a fraud, it will undo all your hard work.

4. **Network as a team.** When employees network for you and tell people about your brand, it's just as valuable as their time spent at a desk. Encourage your employees to get out there and talk. You never know who might be introduced to your brand and become a loyal customer.

5. **Offer assistance to everyone, without expecting anything in return.** Networking 101 suggests that offering a favour, with nothing expected in return, is a good way to build connections. It certainly will make you stand out from the crowd. So extend an offer of help to someone, and make it clear that it comes with no strings. Those acts of kindness will soon add up.

6. **Be adaptable.** Remember that needs and wants change over time as well. Your original tribe might split into smaller ones. Predicting what the consumer landscape will look like in a few years is a useful skill to have.

When building your brand, don't forget to cultivate your tribe. Make sure they are inspired enough to go out there and spread the word about your brand. That's how you can naturally build buzz around your business, without breaking the bank with an expensive marketing campaign. Your brand is more than a logo or colour scheme; it's also about the people around it, the tribe who are willing to shout about you. They are louder than any ad could be.

LEADERSHIP

Tribe Leadership and Your Brand

Building a tribe is the best way to gain customer loyalty over a long time. It mobilizes people to connect more deeply with your brand and might even create a movement. Just look at the loyalty that artists like Little Mix and One Direction inspire in their fans. When they release a new single or album, it practically markets itself.

But a tribe isn't anything without leadership. That is, to lead with the customer always in mind. Your customer needs to be the heart and soul of your organization. That's what will set your company apart from the rest.

Customer First

Tribal leadership marketing should be present throughout your organization. You need to provide your customers with a positive experience at every single touchpoint, including purchasing, post-sale, and every other time they interact with your business. By providing a great (and consistent) experience across all your digital and offline channels, you increase customer loyalty and trust in your brand. Both are the building blocks for a tribe.

In fact, becoming more digitally native and putting the customer first are closely linked. In 2015, Econsultancy asked business leaders about their priorities when creating a "digital-native" culture, and 58 per cent said they intended to become more customer-centric.

Every Stage Counts

Every time customers see your brand, you have an opportunity to convert them to your tribe. From when they find your organization, to the moment they buy from you, through to post-purchase. During this process, you need to convince them not just to like your brand, but to love it.

Share Your Vision

A lot of that comes down to sharing a vision with them. Make people feel like they are part of something bigger.

Did you know that the Bill & Melinda Gates Foundation was rated above YouTube in the World Value Index? It signals a move towards more fulfilling brands. Today's consumers don't just want to connect with a business; they want to change the world.

Consumers have become much more selective about the brands they use. Some brands especially find millennials tricky to connect with, compared to older generations. Therefore, there's a pressing need for brands to provide a tangible benefit and show a purpose in the world.

Why Tribe Leadership?

That's where tribe leadership comes in. By creating and leading your tribe, you resonate with your customers much more than a simple, everyday brand. It's about truly understanding your customers, perhaps more than they know themselves. You need to anticipate their needs in advance and delight them with products and services they might not have considered before. This is a tactic that Amazon often uses. Products are recommended at nearly every stage of the customer journey.

Characteristics of Tribe Leaders

What sets tribe leadership brands apart from the rest is the following:

- Passion. These brands love their customers. They exist solely for their customers and strive to see the world from their customers' perspective. Customer insights and data are incredibly important and used across the entire organization.

- Focus. Products and services are always designed with the customer at the core.

- Relationships. They build relationships to improve the customer experience.

- Strategy. Their customer service strategy seeks to build a tribe by inspiring deeper relationships, trust, and loyalty.

Every Employee

A tribe leader cannot lead alone. Great tribe leadership involves every employee in your company. Everyone must think like a marketer, an innovator, a salesperson, and a customer service rep. Your employees are the face of your brand. They are the people your tribe will interact with every day. Therefore, your employees need to be on board with your brand's mission and vision. Every engagement needs to leave a lasting impression.

Plus, they need to work together. Too often, different departments are only focused on their own goals and challenges. However, in order for tribe leadership to work, you need to break down these organizational silos.

More than Sales

Tribe leadership recognizes that customers are not just sales. It seeks to build relationships over the long term, between the company and customers, and also between the company and employees. To become a tribe leader, you have to inspire everyone in your organization to work together in a customer-centric way. Every second you have with your customers is vital. It's an opportunity to recruit them into your tribe.

A tribe is the ultimate way to develop brand loyalty. Your customers are the key members of your tribe. Put them first in all your decisions, and you'll soon find willing tribe members.

"Pimp My Ride" *

> Trust is like a vase. Once it's broken, though you
> can fix it, the vase will never be same again.
>
> —Walter Anderson

*Reference to a show on Discovery about custom made cars

What Are Your Passion Points and Strengths?

Strong brands don't just happen. They are the results of a long-term strategy that guides how a company does business and is tightly bound to its understanding of customer needs. Companies have to be obsessed with delivering a customer experience in line with the customer's expectations.

In a world where people deliberately block out businesses that they don't trust or appreciate, the key to success is showing your target audience that you're worth their time.

One study in 2016 that looked into the link between transparency and trust found that more than half of consumers consider "additional information" to be important when they're choosing a brand. What's more, 73 per cent of those people would spend more money on a product that offers complete transparency. If that's not enough to showcase the art of honesty, how about the fact that 78 per cent of customers consider brand transparency to be very important, while 70 per cent devote extra time to finding out more about the organizations they buy from?

Ultimately, brand transparency is all about convincing your customer to trust you. Only after you've developed trust can you begin to cultivate the holy grail of great marketing: brand loyalty and brand ambassadors, your tribe.

Customer trust was never easy to win, per se, but it has also never been this difficult. We have entered an era of distrust, due to a perfect storm of different factors.

The excessive amount of misleading advertising is partially to blame. Only 4 per cent of Americans believe that the marketing industry acts with integrity, and the remainder are sceptical of advertisers' intentions. They know companies are out for a profit and are willing to bend the truth to get it. Recent research has found that millennials are less trusting of others than any other generation.

Also, we live in a capitalistic society that strongly encourages individual achievement. For better or worse, those conditions force consumers to look out for themselves and not always be generous toward others.

The digital era has millions of businesses all clamouring for attention. The massive content overload makes it harder to figure out what's real and what isn't.

And then there's fake news. Of course, the recent (and ongoing) fake news epidemic is also meddling with consumers' trust. Everything is to be doubted, and nothing is to be believed.

These days, brand transparency isn't just a nice thing for your company to strive for; it's a crucial part of success. As trust becomes increasingly difficult to attain, brands can differentiate themselves by committing to absolute transparency.

Here are seven things you need to consider to build trust:

1. **Be accessible.** Be available to your customers, and allow them to interact with you. Customers often have questions, and if there's nowhere for them to for answers, or you don't respond in a timely manner, you could lose credibility.

2. **Have a reliable product.** People tend to buy on emotion, not logic. The challenge your business faces is that when customers receive the product, they need to be impressed with its quality to justify their purchase. Talking a good game but then turning around and selling a low-quality product is sure to draw negative reviews, leading to mistrust and decreased credibility.

3. **Be honest.** Being transparent means recognizing and being open about both your strengths and weaknesses. If your product isn't right for one of your prospects, you should be secure enough to guide that prospect in the right direction, even if that act means

boosting your competitor's bottom line. Honesty shows you care about your customers and their needs, and your willingness to help them gets them the results they're looking for.

4. **Bring value to your client.** Do you put your customers first, or do you put revenue first? People know when they're just a dollar sign to you, and while they may still buy from you if they believe your product solves their needs, this does not build long-term trust or encourage repeat sales.

5. **Maintain consistency.** Maintaining consistency ensures that your prospects and customers know what to expect. Your message should be an extension of your actions and behaviour. If it isn't true to who you are, or you can't deliver on it, you are being inconsistent. Your design should be holistically implemented across your logo, website, social networks, and print materials. It is an easy win that can help you build trust with customers. Your delivery, how you communicate with your target audience, through which channels, and how often are all important.

6. **Display company culture.** What's it like to work at your office? A display of company culture shows you're willing to be honest. It shows that your employees like working at the company and that there are humans behind the business, watching out for the good of the customers.

7. **Own your mistakes.** Made a mistake? Own it. Failed at something? Own it. Customers will respect and trust your company even more when you own up to your mistakes and failures. Humans are fallible, and your brand should be, too. And do it quickly. You've got to own up to the mistake before your customers think you're trying to hide it.

While being honest doesn't seem like a big commitment from a consumer perspective, it's something that can be incredibly difficult for businesses, particularly since sharing negative reviews or market information can be enough to lose valuable points for your reputation. However, it's important to remember that transparency is the key to long-term loyalty. The more your customers know about you, your successes, and your failures, the stronger their relationship with your brand will become. Empower your customer to understand your business, and you'll also encourage them to fall in love with your brand.

Honesty is a lonely word.

Obey the principles without being bound by them.

—Bruce Lee

CHAPTER 7

PRINCIPLES

Principles

A principle is a concept or value that is a guide for behaviour or evaluation. According to Cambridge Dictionary, a principle is a basic idea or rule that explains or controls how something happens or works.

I often refer to Harrington Emerson, who said, "As to methods there may be a million and then some, but principles are few. The man who grasps principles can successfully select his own methods. The man who tries methods, ignoring principles, is sure to have trouble."

Marketing is defined as "the total of activities involved in the transfer of goods from the producer or seller to the consumer or buyer," or as Wikipedia defines it, "Marketing is the study and management of exchange relationships. It is the business process of identifying, anticipating and satisfying customers' needs and wants. Because marketing is used to attract customers, it is one of the primary components of business management and commerce." In other words, marketing is all activities that you do to prepare for sales. It is vital for us to understand the principles of marketing and its place in the world. Understanding and applying these principles is essential to defining and applying them to the right methods for success.

Let me explain: Over the years, I have worked with small clients, big clients, unknowns, and globally known brands, and I've discovered that the rule of convenience is ever present in a lot of companies. The fact is, there are so many that look for the quick fix, for simple ways to get some short-term results, not willing to put in the work and build that strong foundation before applying methods to their marketing tactics.

Think about it: All the sales experts and others out there all focus on the methods you should apply, the tactics on how to have success with your marketing activities, lead magnets, and Facebook advertising, and yet ignoring the basics. If you don't invest the hours and resources to really figure out the why, how, what, who, and when, by applying the principles of marketing, you will spend a lot of money and time on stuff that might give you a quick bang for the buck, but it won't be sustainable over time. So in the end, your company, your brand, your employees, and your customers will suffer, and you as the entrepreneur will end up hitting the infamous wall. So here are my thoughts:

My marketing principles are a culmination of thirty years' experience in the marketing industry. The interesting thing, though, was that I always started with the why: What is the purpose, and what are we trying to achieve? What is the business target? Who are we trying to convince, and why are they not doing so today? What are the barriers, what are the drivers, and how can marketing play a part in changing their behaviour?

Then let's revisit the principles of *Brand You Economics*:

Brand, which simply put is people's perception of a company, organization, product, or service. Simply put (I will refer to this later as well), it is a person's gut feeling about said company, organization, product, or service.

You, the brandividual, gatekeeper, influencer, category expert, who exchanges services because you use your channels to produce content, that you distribute and sell to engage and delight your target audience, so you become an economic agent of sorts, that exchanges services with the brand.

Economics is the study of the social science connected to production, distribution, and consumption of goods and services. And the principles of economics focus on how economies work and the behaviours and interactions of economic agents.

So as I mentioned previously, you (people) behave as a brand, and brands behave as you (people), in the economic system that affects the bottom line based on tangible and intangible (soft and factual) values.

Then we need to talk about the touchpoints, the Customer Journey; my Find, Like, Love methodology, that I have used so many times.

Let's go through my four pillars of marketing:

1) **Insight.** This is the data, the context if you will, about the five Cs; your company, competition, category, channels, and customer.

2) **Ambition.** What are your goals and objectives? How do you apply said insight to affect behaviours and outcomes?

3) **Touchpoints.** Really dig down on where your customer is, and find the touchpoints where you can connect on a contextual, cultural, and community level.

4) **Blueprint.** What role will communication play (the tone of voice, visual elements, and assets to make all the above points come to play)?

You can't build a house, a relationship, a company, or a brand without a solid foundation, without defining the bases of where you are and where you want to go. That is the only way you are going to be able to navigate. You need to know point A before you can reach point B. It's that simple and yet so complicated, or not really complicated; it just requires hard work. The reason why it is neglected is because it seems tedious, and you, well, everybody knows, right? So no need to do that boring strategy part; let's just make some Facebook ads, create some variations, and see which performs better, and voila: We are all good.

Sorry, but no. You need to start with the principles, the basics: Define the purpose of your company, brand, product, or service. What type of category are you part of? Who are your competitors? Which channels are most relevant, and who are your customers? What are their needs and wants? What is their behaviour, and how can you influence that behaviour? Are there cultural or contextual considerations? Is there a community we can work with?

Start with these important questions, and you'll soon realize that creating a foundation based on solid principles will enable you to build methods and tactical assets that will be far more effective and build a brand that is going to last for decades.

DEFINE YOUR GOAL

Purpose

Here is the first set of principles in marketing: insight. That's right, this is where you first need to deep dive into the five Cs: Company, Category, Competition, Channels, and Customer. This is what I define as the context for the insight that will end up defining you and your company's ambition or purpose. Because this is the one pillar where your communication platform will be built upon, and if you don't have the details surrounding the five Cs, you're in trouble.

Now, I know you may be thinking, *Pfffff, I know my company and what we stand for, and I know the category we operate in. Heck, competition? We don't have any real competition because we're unique. Channels? We use Facebook, and that works fine, and our customers are the ones that buy from us. Done. What's next?*

Okay, perhaps I am being a bit oversimplified and dumbing down what people think (not you, of course), but you'd be surprised. I have many clients who think they know all of this, or it is the complete opposite, where they just exist, and it works, so who cares? Well, there's a reason why there are marketing agencies and consultants, and that's because this is important. It can result in a huge difference to your bottom line.

The thing is, without the necessary context and insight, you are sort of lost because you are basing your decisions on presumptions and not facts. You should sit down and list all the details about your company, the most important being purpose. What is your company's purpose? What is the reason you exist? What is your unique selling proposition? What is your profit margin? What is your acquisition cost/goal? What is the lifetime value of a client? What is your marketing budget and ROI? What do you define as success? What do you define as failure in your marketing?

And those are only a few trigger questions for the first C: Company. Now you need to map out the same for the other four Cs: Category, Competition, Channels, and Customers. You might think you have the answers in your brain, but unless you put it down on a piece of paper or type it on your computer, essential details can and will be lost, and these details are what make you stand out from the nonexisting competition (ha ha, just kidding; they are right behind you, or in front of you. What do I know? You should, though, right?).

What's next? Category. So ask yourself, in which category do you fit: manufacturer, consumer, retailer? How big is the penetration in these categories by units, sales, margins? Are they growing or declining? What are the key trends in these categories? Can any of them hinder or help your success? What are the most important metrics to your category and why?

Now, let's move into a fun one: Competition. Who is your direct competition? Who is your indirect competition? Any new players you need to defend against? What are their prices? How do they promote their products? What's their tone? Who do they target? Do we know their budgets for marketing spending? How many units do they sell?

Next, we have Channels. Where is the product or service sold? How is the product or service sold? Does the market share depend on distribution channels? Are any critical to success? Do you know of any key trends in sales channels to be aware of? What do the channels think of your brand, product, or service? How can the product be better positioned?

Lastly, we have Consumer. Which consumer segment does the product or service appeal to? How big are they in terms of people, sales, margins? Are they growing or declining? Who are they? What do they love or hate about the brand? What do they love or hate about the competition? What are their thoughts about the product? What are their needs? Wants? Desires?

Once you have mapped out the five Cs, you can dig into specific hypotheses you want to test, based on what you come up with from the session.

- Are you in the right category, or do others have more potential?
- Are there any trends to take advantage of to win?
- How do you beat the competition?
- Why are you remarkable? What makes your offering different?
- Are there any channels where the consumer is more active that you haven't explored?

Okay. Again, as you gather more data and information about the five Cs, you will discover things you hadn't thought of, small details, and they will trigger your brain to suddenly come up with new ideas and tactics that can be implemented.

However, don't jump there just yet. I have a lot more to share with you, so start with gathering the context and insights that you can under each of the five Cs; take a break for a few hours and then revisit the document. You'll be able to add a few more under each one, I'm sure. Once that is done, you will have a solid foundation for where to go next. Now, this document will be super important for you, as it will give you a clear picture of your brand as a whole.

Purpose/Mission/Goal

So here's your brand's purpose or ambition. It sounds like a big word: ambition. Why are we here, where are we now, where are we going, and what is all this for? Well, the last part you also should know. I do hope you know the purpose of your brand, right? Let's talk about how to define *ambition*.

You see, the brand purpose is that big hairy goal of your company or brand, the whole reason for being, and that is very important to have in place before anything else. Now I'm guessing you have something great jotted down for your brand, just like Apple's purpose is simply "To empower creative exploration and self-expression" (amazing, right?), but then, how do you apply that to everyday life? How can that be activated in your business?

That's where ambition comes in. The ambition is, simply put, your two- or three-year plan: What do you want to achieve over the next couple of years? Now, that will give you a clear picture of where you want to go; it's kind of a road map into the future. Which is why it's the ambition of your brand, because you never know what's going to happen, but you can prepare yourself as best as possible.

After you have a clear set of insights, the five Cs, you then move on to the ambition, where you drill down on the goals and objectives. And yes, there is a difference.

Goals, for one, should be ambitious. They should be on the furthest edge of the extremes, something that is almost impossible to achieve, keyword being "almost."

Objectives, on the other hand, are the tasks and milestones that will take you one step at the time towards the goal. You should aim to distil the insights you have gathered into a simple, specific, and sharp description of the ambition. It can be helpful to think of this as "Achieve X, by Y, instead of Z." Where X is a specific goal (growth, defence, etc.), Y is your objectives, your milestones per se, and Z is the status quo or another more obvious course of action.

Defining a tangible ambition for your brand makes it easier to tackle the day-to-day marketing tactics, because now you know the context of your brand, where you are, where you are going, and how you will get there.

Permission

So far, we have covered insights and ambition, and now we are getting into the juicy stuff: human behaviour, what makes people tick. I am talking about your brand's touchpoints, where you need to dig down to determine where your customer is and the touchpoints where you can connect on a contextual, cultural, and community level.

Before we can figure out how to connect with our tribe, we need to figure out what makes people do what they do. This means we need to map out the customer journey. I use my own methodology for this, a three-stage process I call the Find, Like, Love model. I've talked about this multiple times, and now I will give you what's needed for you to create one for your brand. So the three stages are about where the customer is, and what is needed to make a decision.

The customer journey is challenging because of all the different touchpoints that are out there at the moment; how do you tackle them properly? Back in the day, when I first started out in this wonderful world of marketing, there was the AIDA model: Attention, Interest, Decision, and Action (the customer journey of the time).

Now **my Find, Like, Love** model might seem too simple, but it touches on these points: **Find** deals with awareness and engagement, **Like** deals with purchasing and acceptance, **Love** deals with satisfaction and delight. This should be an infinity loop. Before, the focus was just about getting a customer to buy, now it is about building a relationship so that you'll have a loyal, returning customer who stays for as long as possible, because they are delighted to be in a relationship with your brand. Let me explain what you need to map out for the customer journey:

Touchpoints, meaning where you reach your consumers, existing ones and new ones. What are their trigger points, their drivers and barriers? How can communication change or affect their behaviour so they become a new customer or return and buy more from you.

So think of the **Find** stage as the place where you are talking to strangers; they know nothing about you or your brand. So how do you engage with them? How do you make them aware? Well, do you solve a problem? If you do, then you have your driver, but isn't this problem addressed by other brands as well? Or perhaps they are scared of testing something new? There's your barrier; now think about how you can reduce the barrier and motivate the driver. That's the message.

Okay, so they go from being a stranger to becoming your customer; they've gone from **Find** to **Like** because they wouldn't become a customer if they didn't like your brand, product, or service, right? Okay, again, think about the same things: What is the driver for them to use the product or service? What is the barrier? And what can you say (message) to change their behaviour? In this stage, it is about the experience of using the product or service, the packaging, the instructions, the material, the tone, and so on.

In the last stage, they knew about you and bought from you, and now, you need to figure out how to make them **love** you, to be delighted enough so they recommend you to their network and stay with you over time, becoming loyal and returning customers. It's like I said, think of it as a relationship; it needs to be taken care of and maintained. The grass isn't greener on the other side if you make sure to take great care of your own grass, right? So make sure your customers know this and feel it.

The only way to make sure you are handling them properly is by mapping out the customer journey, because then you know the touchpoints for your marketing and how you can influence their behaviour into entering a long-term relationship with you and your brand.

One Rule to Rule Them All

We have gone through the principles of marketing and *Brand You Economics*. As previously mentioned, the pillars of *Brand You Economics*; interactions; perceptions; and behaviours are all linked to financial performance based on the total value of the customer, conversion rate, conversion time, all to understand the brand value better.

But as we have gone through the principles and pillars, we need a way to think, measure, and tangibly apply them so your brand stands out and captures the interactions, perceptions, and behaviours of your audience.

That's where the one rule to rule them all comes into play. I have used this myself on all campaigns, concepts, and assets made over the years. It is so simple, and yet so many companies, even agencies and professionals, forget to check their tactics and assets against it. The thing is, when you try to communicate with your target audience, there is so much you want to say, so many unique and compelling reasons, facts, and things you want to communicate about your brand, product, or service, all the things that are important to you, but to them, they don't really care (yet) or even are capable to take in all that information. To them, they want the hook, then the one thing that separates you from everyone else. Granted, it could be something benign such as price, colour, weight, physical appearance, texture, fabric, and so on. And then, when you are about to figure out what to say, it all comes pouring out, and it becomes hard to figure out how to navigate. For one, remember it is not about you, but them.

Now it is time for me to reveal to you the simple yet magical formula you need to apply when considering the assets and tactical marketing activities you want to do:

1rE2zag

Now, I am pretty sure you are thinking, *What the hell does this gibberish mean, and how am I to apply it to my marketing assets?*

Let me explain:

1

Make sure you have one message, and only one. Not two, not five, but one clear message. The one thing you want your target audience to pay attention to.

Picture this: It's a beautiful Sunday morning. You are in the kitchen and want to make a delicious omelette with your partner. So you get the bowl and tools to whisk things together, and your better half goes to the fridge and, deciding to be a bit playful this morning, tosses you the eggs and tells you to catch them.

Freeze-frame; okay, two scenarios are to be played out:

One, your partner tosses you five eggs, all at once. Let's just assume you are a normal human, and not a circus artist of sorts, so the panic that arises in your brain as you try to catch all of them is vivid and terrifying. In the complete stress and confusion of the situation, you don't manage to catch any of them, and they all fall smack to the floor and make a mess to clean up. Plus, no omelette, as those were the last five eggs you had.

Now, let's try that again with the second scenario: This time, your partner tosses the eggs to you, one by one. Most likely, you will catch all of them, easily, or maybe one will fall to the ground, giving you both a bit of a laugh, but you still caught four out of five eggs, so you can make that delicious omelette. You both are very satisfied and pleased with the morning.

It's safe to say that by focusing on one message at a time, it will make it easier for the receiver to grasp, take in, and act upon whatever you want them to, agreed?

Case Study: Absolut Vodka

Despite having no distinct shape, Absolut made their iconic vodka bottle the most recognizable bottle in the world. Their "In the Wild" campaign, which featured print ads showing the bottle shape in various ways around the world, was so successful that they didn't stop running it for twenty-five years, being the longest uninterrupted ad campaign ever, featuring more than fifteen hundred separate ads. Why change a working formula, right?

When the campaign started, their market share was below 2.5 per cent. By the late 2000s, when the campaign was ended, Absolut was importing 4.5 million cases per year, or half of all imported vodka in the US.

Why It's Important

It doesn't matter if your product looks boring; you can still tell your story in a compelling way. Again: Absolut created fifteen hundred ads about a bottle. One message. It's that simple.

Okey, the next part of the formula:

R

Make sure your message is relevant, which means, in all simplicity, know your audience. So when you go out with a brand message, that one thing, you also need to make sure you are speaking to them about what they care about. If they are complete strangers to you, then it comes down to segmentation, based on demographics, geography, and psychographics. But if this is your tribe (remember bonfire marketing from chapter 6) you are talking to, make sure you are on point. If they are used to you speaking about apples for as long as they've been part of your brand journey, you can't just drop on them oranges; remember, they are there to hear about apples. So make sure your message, that one message, is relevant.

Case Study: Dove

Dove's #RealBeauty campaign pioneered self-esteem and self-love; heck, it even became the brand's mission. In 2004, Dove discovered that only 2 per cent of women in their research groups considered themselves beautiful. As a result, the company created a campaign with messages about inner beauty, authenticity, and female empowerment.

Dove's campaign ads spoke directly to their customers. They even pledged to stop all retouching across their marketing in 2018, which earned the brand a lot of attention and credibility.

Some methods they applied:

Dove and Twitter ad teams partnered up to identify and respond to negative tweets about beauty and body image (#SpeakBeautiful campaign).

Dove flooded Shutterstock with photographs of normal, real women tagged "beautiful," all taken by award-winning photographers, and encouraged others to do the same.

Dove and Getty Images created five thousand images of underrepresented women, free for public use.

Why It's Important

In the Prophet Brand Relevance Index (BRI), Dove remains the most relevant brand in the Household & Personal category (increasing its lead every year), and they are placed in the top ten of all brands in the Customer Obsession category. Keeping it real and keeping the message relevant.

So next, we have:

E2

Engaging and emotional. Let's break them down into two separate components. First, emotional; 70 per cent of all purchasing decisions are based on emotion with the decision maker. If we add in subconscious processes, we are sometimes close to 95 per cent, according to studies. What does it mean? Well, it's all about how what we see, touch, smell, hear, or taste makes us feel in the moment. So in your case, if it is a digital asset for your brand, it will only come down to a few of the senses, but if it is a physical one, it activates all the senses, which can be both a pro and a con. Anyways, the senses will evoke an emotion, and the feeling that arises will determine if they will be open and prone to act, but there is no doubt that emotional content moves consumers in a way that makes it easier for them to relate and take action.

Which leads us to the second component, the engaging part. Do receivers get enough information to act, or will they be left with more questions that prevent them from taking action? Will they care? Will they be moved or touched, in some shape or form? These are also important issues to consider in the design of your assets.

Now, the combination of engaging and emotional will also make some impression on how credible your brand is perceived to be, as the messaging and emotional content, combined with the level of engagement, will give them a strong impression of whether you can be trusted or not. You know the saying, if something is too good to be true, it probably is. Make sure your message is honest and that you are as credible and trustworthy as possible.

Case Study: VW

Volkswagen's "Think Small" campaign is the definition of a millennial campaign. Created in 1960 by Doyle Dane & Bernbach (DDB), the campaign set out to answer one question: How do you change peoples' perceptions not only about a product, but also about an entire group of people?

Americans always had a propensity to buy big American cars, and even fifteen years after World War II ended, few Americans were buying small German cars. But the economy was struggling, as repairs of those big American cars were pricy and also had to be done by dealerships, plus gasoline was expensive.

The VW Beetle was the complete opposite: low gas consumption, easy to fix yourself, and with cheap parts. So what did this Volkswagen advertisement do? It played right into the audience's expectations. You think I'm small? Yeah, I am. They never tried to be something they were not, but they did it in a very simple, compelling way.

Why It's Important

Don't try to sell your company, product, or service as something it is not. Consumers recognize and appreciate honesty, and that is created by engaging and emotional stories.

So for the final component:

Zag

Marty Neumeyer, the author of the book *Brand Gap*, wrote the following: "Today you have to out-position, out-manoeuvre, and out-design the competition."

The new rule? When everyone zigs, you zag. Or as Seth Godin abundantly made clear in his book *The Purple Cow*, you have to be remarkable.

Now, there is a misconception about the word *remarkable*, as some believe it means to be outstanding, unique, a unicorn of sorts, which is not the case. It is made of the words *remark* and *able*, meaning someone finds something interesting and different enough so they talk about it; they make a remark about it to their family, friends, and network.

So to summarize, when you make tactical assets to promote and make people aware of your brand, product, or service, it needs to have one message, that they perceive to be relevant, that engages them and is emotional, so they feel that it is worth talking about and spreading.

Case Study: Google

Google Creative Lab, working with BBH, unveiled a now-classic spot for the then-three-year-old Chrome browser. The campaign humanized the company and lent warmth to a cold tech product through a story of love, told through behind-the-scenes captures and family memories. This campaign was about a father's love for his daughter, and the digital scrapbook he kept about her life, thanks to Google products.

It was called "Dear Sophie."

Most people really just think of Google as a technology company, and they did a masterful job of placing their purpose of being in this life story. It wasn't forced. It wasn't like they were making stuff up. You can say whatever you want about technology; sure, it can be used to do bad, but it can also be used to create wonder and magic. So in my opinion, this is a brand that managed to step outside their own bubble of thinking features and instead focused on you, their users, and the benefits of using their products and services. In my opinion, it was a remarkable way to get into people's hearts and minds, without talking about the product.

Why It's Important

The perfect marketing concept has one message that is relevant, engaging, and emotional, and it stands out in a honest and real way. I remember when I saw this ad, my first reaction was, "Damn, I wish I created this ad, and damn, I wish I did what the dad did in this ad."

Google "Dear Sophie" and write to me on dearsophie@ brandyoueconomics.com and tell me if I am right, or if you have a better example. I'd love to hear from you.

Focus on the Horizon

Okay, I have gone through a lot of material and covered a lot of ground to prepare you to learn how to make your brand stand out with effective marketing. I hope I have made crystal clear that you can't think short-term, instant fixes and gratification; instead, you must focus on the long game, the horizon. You are a brand, so you need that gut feeling people have when they think of you to be as good, solid, credible, and positive as possible.

I have warned about this many times. So many of people forget to do the groundwork, planning and strategy, and they just jump to the making of assets and put it out there to see if someone, anyone buys what they are offering.

If you want to succeed with your brand, you need to keep your eyes on the horizon; why did you get into this business in the first place? I know why I did it; my vision statement, my purpose is "to use my curiosity, passion, and knowledge that makes a positive impact on people around me, and I do that by simplifying the complexity of marketing by creating stories that sell." That is my why, how, and what. Don't forget. Make it stick, and remind yourself about your horizon,

Now this has to come across in all channels, and all the messaging, tone, and assets you make for your brand and what you are all about.

Let me explain.

The purpose of life is to
contribute in some way
to make things better.

—Robert F. Kennedy

CHAPTER 8

CONCLUSION

Wrapping Things Up

So you have now completed the chapters containing the best information, advice, tactics, and tools I have to offer. I hope you've enjoyed reading it as much as I've enjoyed writing it. I also hope you feel better prepared for what is needed to build a legacy brand based on *Brand You Economics*. It has been a privilege to have your attention and to be granted the honour and opportunity to inspire, lead, and guide you with my passion, curiosity, and knowledge.

I will now sum up this book into some short and tangible paragraphs as a quick reference for you to return to, without needing to go back and read it all over again; you can, of course, and should, once in a while, but for a quick reminder, this conclusion should do the trick and get you back on track.

Purpose

Always start with why.

Earlier, I mentioned William Barclay, who said there were two great days in someone's life: The day they were born, and the day they discovered why.

Your purpose is why you do what you do every morning. It is fulfilling and gives you a true sense of accomplishment, joy, and success. Purpose drives action, and it has to start from the top and be infused in every touchpoint of the brand, internally and externally. Giving your brand a purpose doesn't just affect your employees; it can also motivate your customers into feeling like they are having an impact on the world.

If you asked a random person on the street, "Who are you, and why should I care?" your answer should be clear and consistent.

We are in the purpose-driven era; brands whose why is weaved into their fabric will outpace other brands. It attracts more people, your people, your tribe, and it will make you profitable and make a positive change to the world.

Speaking of …

People

As a marketer, you need to be aware of what drives the people you try to reach, what stops them from doing what you ask of them, and how to trigger the desired response or behaviour. But before you come to that stage of the process, you need to find your audience, your people, your tribe.

In short, this knowledge of your target audience will drive your entire marketing strategy—your product, pricing, promotion, and positioning. Defining your target audience will help you avoid wasting resources like time, money, and personnel that are precious to any company. There's an old saying by Confucius that comes to mind in this scenario: "The man who chases **two rabbits**, catches neither." So knowing exactly who you want to chase is key. I mean, even the smallest niche market has plenty of people to serve, but try to get them all, and you'll likely end up with nothing.

1. **Define your niche.** What is the one thing you are most passionate about in regards to your business of choice? Define that one thing, and bring your A-game. The energy and engagement will shine through your content and will make you interesting to the audience you seek.

2. **What do you want?** More specifically, what do you want them to do? Buy your product? One specific item, or add more products to their basket? Become a recurring customer? Share your content? Sign up for a newsletter? What is the one thing you want to change in their behaviour? This insight will define who you are targeting and their behaviour.

3. **Find your heroes.** How are your competitors or similar businesses doing? Is there any type of innovation happening in your category, the niche you need to be aware of? How do they engage, communicate, and advertise their business? Learn from them, and adapt your strategy.

4. **Listen.** This is the most underestimated word of all. The Internet is the place to gather information and find truths about your audience. Start with what you know, the simple stuff: demographics, then move on to psychographics; interests, hobbies, and passions. How do they spend their time and money? What blogs, newspapers, and magazines do they read? What is their favourite food and movie? What social media networks do they access? What do they do on weekends? These important questions need to be answered so you can meet their needs and solve their problems.

5. **Attract the gatekeepers.** Once you know a bit more because you listened, it's time to engage, look around, and find the gatekeepers and influencers who are active within your niche. If you get the gatekeepers to get onboard, you've come a long way.

If they like what you have to offer, they will grant you access to their tribe, and you are a step closer.

Your entire marketing strategy—from product to pricing to promotion to positioning—rests on the shoulders of your insight about your tribe, their primary drivers, and their barriers, so you are able to define the desired response or the behavioural change you want. If you can't connect with, appeal to, and solve a problem for them, you will fail.

Become a Brand That Leads

Tribe leadership marketing is the discipline of doing business with your customer in a way that provides a positive customer experience before and after the sale in order to drive repeat business, maintain customer loyalty, and increase profits.

Tribe leadership is not just about offering great customer service; it means offering a great experience from the Find stage, through the purchasing process or Like stage, and finally through the post-purchase process, the Love stage. It's a strategy that's based on putting your customers first and keeping them at the core of your business. Tribe leadership is all about sharing a vision; inspire your tribe, and together you will achieve the impossible.

By embracing tribe leadership marketing, you anticipate customers' needs and delight them with products and services they may not have thought of but will immediately fall in love with. That means you create products, processes, policies, and a culture that is designed to support customers with a great experience as they are working towards their goals. Brands that stand out regarding tribe leadership are committed to the following four practices:

1. They are passionate and truly believe the customer comes first. They believe that without the customer, they cannot succeed in business (which is true), and they want to see the world through the customer's eyes. Marketers inside these organizations understand what customers want and use customer data to capture and share insights across the organization.

2. After focusing on what the customer wants and needs, they develop products and services around that.

3. They focus on building relationships designed to maximize the customer's product and service experience.

4. They analyse, plan, and implement a carefully formulated customer strategy that focuses on creating and keeping profitable and loyal customers. In short, their tribe.

Tribe leadership also means that the brand needs to instil a mindset that every employee should think like a marketer, an innovator, a salesperson, and a customer service representative, as each touchpoint with your tribe is an opportunity to meet their needs. It is essential to build experiences (digital or human) that are genuine and transparent. The fact is, employees are the face and voice of a brand, and each interaction has a lasting impact on customer perception.

Make Them Stick Around

The tribe are your customers, and the bonfire is the platform where you inform, enlighten, and entertain them; it sounds pretty easy, right? Well, if you don't have compelling stories, the tribe will leave and find better places to be, and if you don't maintain the bonfire, adding wood and making sure it has that long, swirling, and captivating burn, they will leave as the conversations fade and go cold.

Seth Godin defines a tribe as "a group of people connecting to a leader, to an idea, and to each other." He says a tribe only needs two things: a shared interest and a way to communicate.

A Place to Connect

Empathy. Could this story be about me? Empathy isn't just telling a story that interests people. It's telling a story of interest that they can easily imagine themselves being part of. To do this, you need to ask, "What interests my target audience?" not "What do I want to tell them?"

Personalization. Has this happened to a real person? People not only connect to good stories; they remember and retell them. If you make your customers the heroes of the stories you tell them, your products will sell themselves.

Memorability. Is there something remarkable about this story?

To obtain an effective bonfire conversation, you need

- to show up (you need a place to have a bonfire),
- to communicate (you need to light your fire), and
- consistency (don't let your fire burn out).

Bonfire marketing is about creating that community where you inform, enlighten, and entertain your tribe. Keep showing up, communicate with a consistent voice, and tell different stories around your passion points and beliefs. They will stick around for a lifetime.

One of the smartest marketers I know – Seth Godin – once said, "Leadership is the art of giving people a platform for spreading ideas that work."

Principles

This book has been discussing the principles of *Brand You Economics* and my own principles, as well as the one rule, and by following these principles, you will be better set for the future and for building that legacy brand you so want to create and achieve.

Brand You Economics follows principles built on the interactions, perceptions, and behaviours of your brand, that is, ending up in the sum, the value, be it soft or hard values. At the end of the day, it is the growth and monetary results that will keep you in business, but the soft values, the intangible values, will matter more to your employees, who believe in your brand and support its purpose, as well as the customers, your tribe, which will believe in being part of something that makes this world a better place (intent→ action).

In short, *Brand You Economics* is the study of all things that influence and impact a brand performance and how it affects the bottom line.

Let's summarize the principles of *Brand You Economics*:

1. **Interaction.** When you know the people, your target audience, your tribe, you need to map out the interactions you have with them; where can they reach you, what is your tone of voice in the communication, and what is the level of customer engagement and service you provide? This goes beyond marketing.

2. **Perception.** This is imperative because it doesn't matter what your intentions are behind your communication, marketing, or brand message; what matters is how you are perceived and how that affects the interaction with your tribe, but also what type of behaviour you have. This is all about how they feel about your brand.

3. **Behaviour.** Brand economics is based on rational and emotional values, but now there is also a societal value and how your brand

defines its role in the society, so, in short, it's about measuring the gap between intention and action. Make sure it is minimal so that your brand lives up to the promises, values, and purpose.

That ends up in the brand value and ROI of your legacy, and it is just as much about intangible values. Hard to measure. You need to link the performance of the brand to the principles above, plus historical data, so you know the full scope and value of every touchpoint of your brand.

Then my own principles:

1. **Insight.** Gather all the facts and data you can about your company, customers, channels, competition, and the category your brand is part of. Don't assume, know. Makes sure you uncover all truths, even the uncomfortable ones, so you build the brand based on the right premise.

2. **Ambition.** What is the ambition of the brand? What do you want to achieve? What are your goals and objectives? Is the goal big and hairy, yet obtainable? Are your objectives actionable and tangible? Be truthful and honest.

3. **Touchpoints.** This is where my methodology of Find, Like, Love comes to play. What are the touchpoints of your brand? How will you find strangers, or how will they find you? How do you convert them to become customers and accept (and believe) what you have to offer? And finally, how to make them love you, maintain a relationship, be a return customer, and better yet, be a brand advocate or ambassador, bringing new people to your front door based on word of mouth. All this by defining the barriers (Why don't they do what we want?) and drivers (What will make them change their mind?) to change behaviour (communication); it all comes down to understanding

and studying the interactions, perceptions, and behaviour of your tribe.

4. **Blueprint.** What role will be played by communication, tone of voice, visual elements, and assets to make all the above points come to life, with a solid message, that is made to build trust and awareness, which gives you the most desirable feat of them all: attention.

And lastly, the one rule: 1rE2Zag.

Do you remember it? One message, that is relevant, emotional, engaging, and remarkable.

So simple, and yet so challenging to remember on the day to day, because we get caught up on what is happening right in front of us, which makes it tempting to just try something snappy, a quick fix, but please don't. Stay consistent, be aware of why you do what you do, how, what, when, and who.

You are pretty much prepared to construct a solid foundation, a strategy, a platform for your brand that you can apply to the methods of marketing and creative assets.

PERFORMANCE

Understand Your Business

Brand You Economics is about being aware and knowing which category you operate in, who your competitors are, the context of your product or service, as well as a deep understanding of who your customer is and your tribe (I'll repeat this to boredom, ha ha). But the fact is, the only way you can build a legacy brand is to fully understand all aspects of your business: the interactions, the perceptions, and the behaviour that affect your day-to-day business. They say you cannot reach your goals unless you know your status quo. It's the same as reading a map; if you only know your destination, without knowing your location, you are lost.

In all simplicity, you need to have a hard talk with yourself, fully understand your business, and create a road map from that point moving forward. This is how you can reach your *big hairy goal*, through tangible and actionable objectives, because you know where you are and where you are going. It gives you velocity. And velocity is the definition of speed and direction, but hold that thought.

Forecast Your Performance

This is again related back to knowing your goals and objectives. Based on your insight, you can define your ambitions for the brand, and remember to minimize the gap between intent and action. Then you will have no problem setting up a simple forecast on your performance based on hard values (facts) as well as soft values (intangibles) and then defining milestones. This should be focused on the communications blueprint, where you focus on the Find, Like, Love methodology, and in that, map out the barriers, the drivers, and how communication should change behaviour. Then you map out which channel has which function and the end objective, and that is your forecast.

Drive Growth

Growth can be determined in so many ways, and it all boils down to your ambitions. What is it you want? Is it huge sales, revenue, bottom line? Are we talking about the number of offices, outlets, stores, and employees, or are we talking about intangible values: brand affinity, brand impact, sustainability profile, and societal impact? Whatever the end goal might be, you now have the insight, principles, and tools to make it happen. By understanding the principles of *Brand You Economics*, you can build a strong foundation to make a legacy brand, a brand for generations, a brand to be proud of, that achieves the goals you set and moves beyond them.

Marketing

Brilliant marketing is achieved when you have a strategy in place that is built on these principles. *Brand You Economics* guides you, like the North Star, to define the interactions, perceptions, and behaviours that are connected to your brand story, and then when you apply my marketing principles (insight, ambition, touchpoints, and blueprint), you have the proper tools to make magical marketing assets.

And then remember the one rule (to rule them all), and as Harrington Emerson said, "As to methods there may be a million and then some, but principles are few. The man who grasps principles can successfully select his own methods. The man who tries methods, ignoring principles, is sure to have trouble."

I have provided you with the much-needed principles and tangible tools for you to build your legacy brand. So now you can select your methods to apply said principles and tangible tools, and make brilliant marketing that gets the right kind of attention because you have built trust. After understanding your audience and gathering them around the bonfire, you lead them through messages that are consistent, that are built on purpose, and that offer value, and because of that, your tribe, both internally and externally, will be made aware that your brand is a brand of legacy, to be reckoned with, and that will provide value and make them feel part of something that is greater than themselves.

End Note

How do you feel? Intimidated, motivated, inspired, or overwhelmed? Or a little bit of everything? I can assure you, I have been through what you are going through, and then some, just by planning and writing this book. But I do hope I have provided you with some useful insight, tangible tools, and solid principles you can grasp and apply to your brand when creating assets and finding your methods to reach out and engage with your tribe.

This has been a very fun and challenging project, where I have questioned myself time and time again. I have felt exhausted and ignited. I've learned a lot about myself and evolved my knowledge and understanding of marketing and branding as a whole, so I just need to say thank you. Thank you for joining me on this journey, thank you for completing this book, thank you for taking the time to go through these pages with me, which is based on my beliefs, as well as my curiosity, passion, and knowledge accumulated over the past three decades.

I will leave you with this: If you go to http://marketingatheart.com/book/ and leave your name and email address, I will send you a gift that I think you will find valuable as a supplement to this book.

I can also admit that even though it has taken me countless hours, blood, sweat, tears, and quite a few glasses of delicious Barolo (my favourite red wine from Piedmont in Italy), this has given me the drive to create and write more books. I truly enjoy mentoring, sharing, and helping brandividuals and entrepreneurs like yourself to excel, and I hope this book (and perhaps my next ones) will be valuable to your quest.

I will also bring to life a "masters of marketing" class, which is an intermediate to an advanced online class where you as a member of my tribe will get access to video classes, whitepapers, templates, and worksheets, as well as a closed community group of like-minded people, where you'll get one-on-one mentoring sessions, as well as the chance to ask me and the other members questions related to your brand journey and the pains you might be facing.

But for now, just remember: do the work, make the effort, and use this book and all the insight and knowledge that is here to build the proper foundation for your brand, whether you are an influencer wanting to up your game and take it to the next level and monetize your brand, or you are an entrepreneur, a start-up, a scale-up, or a company that is ready for the major league. Understand *Brand You Economics*, follow its principles, and use the tangible tools I have given you, and you are well on your way to creating a legacy brand you'll be proud of.

Hold that thought. ;)

CASE STUDY: DOMINO'S

The Easy Order Button

I guess you know the brand Domino's, the pizza bread? No, wait; they actually define themselves as a technology company that just happens to sell pizza (love this).

Anyway, a few years ago, I worked with Domino's and handled all their marketing efforts in the Nordics. At some point, I was also invited to have a chat with the digital director at Domino's UK, which handled the markets of Great Britain, as well as Benelux and Germany (after the campaign, they took over the Nordics as well).

So in this conversation, we talked about the ideas and concepts I was working with, and as always, I listened, asked questions to get more insight, and gave a few pointers and nudges with ideas that could evolve into a project. And what would you know; that conversation led to me getting a brief from Domino's UK which was a very cool challenge, which I jumped on gladly.

The reason I mention this case is that this is a perfect example of *Brand You Economics*.

So let's just jump into it.

First, the setup, the brief. Domino's asked me to work on a concept that was to introduce their newest app to the UK market. They needed it to have a massive impact, but the budget was limited, so something that could be used in PR would be perfect. The challenge they were facing was the fact that most of the orders to Domino's were made over the phone, despite the fact that they already had a decent website and there was an app that was operational, but, they admitted, it was not working, and people avoided using it. That's why they needed to make a campaign for the updated app, which was easier to use, more secure, and more cool as well. Domino's call centres processed the phone orders at a massive cost and also had the risk of lost payments, cash handling, and so on.

So my brain started working, and I remember I had talked to the team at Domino's about making some sort of physical button, to be given to the local bars, pubs, and social spots. I had this huge chunk of a Wi-Fi button at the office that I thought might do the trick, but I wanted something smaller, easier, and way cooler. So after a few days of research, I came across a start-up in Stockholm called Flic: a small Bluetooth button about an inch in diameter, that connected to an app and you could apply different functions via the smartphone: turn on and off smart lights, Spotify, and other solutions within certain limits, but in general, a pretty hefty device.

So I reached out to the Flic guys and got them to come over and present the concept of this button and how it could work, and a few Flics to use myself. After testing the device and trying different functions, discussing various options with the development team, I started to get an idea of the potential. Then I asked for a quote, the minimum amount to order.

With all the insight in place, it was time to check in with the client and see if they liked the idea. Thankfully, they did, but they also had some additional challenges that made me expand the concept and solution.

I knew we had to find a way to focus on the interactions, look at their customers, figure out their perception of the Domino's brand, and determine how we could change or influence their behaviour. I received quite a lot of insight, data, and facts from the client, then I did a bit of extra digging and assembled a pretty solid piece of work that the client and I believed would do the trick.

Enter the easy order button from Domino's.

Basically, the insight we gathered was that we needed to do something quite remarkable, to influence the loyal users of Domino's that pretty much called in their orders out of habit and convenience, and we knew we didn't have a massive media budget, so we needed to think outside the box (no pun intended).

So I suggested to do an influencer campaign and ship these buttons to 100 selected people and Domino's clients, within sports, gaming, music, and YouTubers. What they were to receive was a package consisting of a small Domino's pizza box, with an easy order button inside, placed in a pizza slice foam cut-out, so the button wouldn't move around inside the box.

Within the box was a letter with information and instructions on how to download the app I designed, following Domino's brand guidelines. Furthermore, they were informed that once they had entered their personal delivery info into the app, the first two orders were going to be free.

Simple, well written, and well executed, it was shipped to those selected influencers in the UK. So what happened over the next two weeks was massive, impressive. The campaign exceeded our wildest expectations. Most of the influencers downloaded the app, selected their favourite pizza, entered their delivery info, linked the easy order button, and made their order almost instantly after receiving the package. On top of that, they posted images and videos to Instagram, Facebook, Twitter, and YouTube, bragging about how cool this was.

One YouTuber in particular made a video for about thirty minutes, bragging about how cool this was; he even filmed the delivery guy arriving with the pizza and then kissed the easy order button box afterwards, because he was so happy with the whole solution. Within a day, the video had more than 160,000 views.

During week two of the campaign, we launched the PR machinery and got featured in ninety-four international media outlets with close to a billion unique impressions. But even though that was impressive, we succeeded with having people calling and requesting to get the physical button; Domino's informed them that they just had to download the new app, as the physical button was not needed. Some targeted ads were done on the followers to the selected influencers, and we had fantastic success with the app entering the top ten list of most downloaded apps in the first week of the launch.

Needless to say, the client was happy, but my takeaway was that we did everything right in the short amount of time we had been given. This campaign is the perfect case that proves that by using the principles of *Brand You Economics* and my own marketing principles and methodology, everything applied beautifully in the customer journey of Find, Like, Love.

We managed to change behaviour by focusing on the interactions and perceptions of the brand. We had the insights, we defined the ambition, the touchpoints were defined, we structured the drivers and barriers, and we knew how the message was going to drive the desired change in behaviour. All this information was entered into the communications blueprint, that then was matched up against the results in the scorecard at the end of the campaign. We measured the results from the different stages of Find, Like, Love, and how the interactions, perceptions, and behaviour changed because of this campaign. The intangible and tangible results were obvious, and the campaign was a success for the Domino's brand. By engaging the influencers and gatekeepers, they changed perceptions as the users went from thinking Domino's was old, traditional, and a bit passé, to become a cool digital brand that transformed and simplified the transaction for the user. But it also made the business more profitable, more secure, and with less churn than before.

We transformed the ordering business of Domino's from the physical analog and chunky process, to a full-on digital and fun activation that improved the bottom line and the brand affinity.

And that, ladies and gentlemen, is how *Brand You Economics* is applied.

Understand the principles, then you can apply your own methods and build a legacy brand, campaign, or activation.

ACKNOWLEDGEMENTS

This book wouldn't have come to life without the inspiration and drive I received from a number of people who were part of my life over the years. It is crazy to think that the skeleton of this book was conceived in a Nero Coffeeshop in London, near Bond Street, where I was waiting and having a coffee, and suddenly it just hit me: I should write a book. Next, what should it be about? And though I hadn't clarified my personal vision, it became this: to use my knowledge, curiosity, and passion to make a positive impact on people around me.

This vision has always been at the core of who I am and what I do. So of course the book had to be about marketing, and of course it had to be about the principles and systems I had accumulated and clarified over the years in various agencies, working with clients, brands, and individuals.

Through my whole career, there have been many influential people I feel worth mentioning: my teachers at the Visual Academy; Robert Ball, my topography teacher, who gave me a love for letters and fonts, and inspired me with the beautiful work of Neville Brody; Peter, who was my arts teacher and taught me all the various techniques: pencil drawing, charcoal, oil paint, watercolour, crayons, airbrush, and more. I've forgotten my photography teacher's name, but he gave me the basic knowledge of how to use a camera, and then my art director teacher, whose scribbling made no sense to me at the time. Being a perfectionist, I wanted every sketch, illustration, composition, and design to be perfect, but he was more about teaching me the importance of getting the idea, the story, down first and then executing it to perfection.

I'd like to share one little story which stuck with me throughout my career: On the final exam of the three-year bachelor's in visual communication, we were given first an illustration exam for Friday, and then a packaging design exam for the following week. I don't know how, but for some reason, I thought exams started on Monday and was relaxing at my parents' place, with the notion that we had said Friday off. Then the phone rang, and it was a classmate, in panic, telling me to get my ass to the academy as fast as possible, or I'd be failed from class.

My parents' house was a ninety-minute drive away, so I just hopped in the car and drove as fast as I could and made it there before 11 a.m., the latest time to arrive and get started. If not, my three years would have been a waste. I arrived at 10.54 and got my assignment, which was to make an illustration for an ad. We could go and find inspiration from our surroundings. We could choose from three different ideas, and I chose one for gym clothes, so my initial thought was to head to the gymnastics hall and see if I could find something to inspire my illustration, but then I was looking at the clock, and I felt I had not enough time. All my classmates were already a few hours ahead of me, so I was feeling the pressure as well. I picked a pile of magazines and started browsing for inspiration, found one, freehand illustrated it, used colour pantone markers to make it look fresh and nice, made the composition for the ad, heading, copy, added a simple logo at the bottom, and boom, two hours later, I delivered the assignment, mounted and wrapped, to my teacher, as the first of my class. I smiled, wished them a good weekend, and headed home to my parents again.

Monday morning, packaging design, and I chose to do one for salmon, by using the technique of airbrush (something I had never done before, but it looked cool). The first three days, I had no idea how my assignment was going to turn out; I was lost, looking for inspiration, looking through books, magazines, Getty Images, and more. Then, Wednesday night, it hit me, the vision, and I started designing. I pushed myself through the next seventy-two hours with no sleep, trying multiple variations of airbrush techniques before I managed to illustrate a salmon that looked nice, finalized the packaging design, and mounted it, wrote a description of my process and explained why I designed it the way I did, and why I thought this was going to work to the end consumer.

I handed in the work three hours before the final deadline and just said to myself, *This is the best work I could do, so hand it in and forget about it.*

A few weeks later, after our exams had been evaluated by creative directors from different advertising agencies in the country, the day of judgement had arrived. All the work was put on display in the main hall, and I was so nervous, because I could see the work of my talented classmates on the walls, and I had no idea what to expect.

But it turned out I ended up with the highest grade for idea, execution, and overall performance. Best in class. Our teachers gathered us to discuss the results and to get people's opinions on the results. One of my classmates, Astrid (I remember her name vividly to this day), stood up and claimed that I should be flunked because I arrived too late for the first day of exam, plus I was the first to leave, so she felt it was unfair I was given the best grade.

The room turned silent for a minute, and everyone looked at me for a reaction. I was just dead silent, speechless as to how someone could think and express such a thing, but okay.

Then my art director teacher, who used to work for some of the bigger agencies, said, "Well, actually, Arnt delivered on point, and before deadline, and our peers have rated his work to be of the highest quality. How do you think it will be to work in agencies once you are out of school? Do you think they will appreciate people who wait until the final minute and/or pass the deadlines every time, or do you think they'd prefer an art director that delivers great work ahead of time? He [me] is ready for the agency world; you are not."

Those words hit me hard and inspired me. It also has been my reminder constantly that perfection is the enemy of the great. Granted, I always push myself to get as close as possible to perfection without compromising the deadline or delivery.

One person in particular, who was an inspiration to me at the academy, but also later in life, when I had the pleasure of calling him a colleague at one of the agencies I've worked at, is Pål Wehus. His creative mind, borderless curiosity, and amazing talent have always been an influence on me, and he still to this day impresses me.

Jan Anderson was the first agency owner who looked at my portfolio; I asked him how to get a job in this industry, and Anderson told me, "Just call, monthly, be persistent, and you'll get a job."

Well, I did; I called him every month for three years, until he gave up and gave me a job as a junior art director. He was a terrifying man to work for, because he had massive standards and impeccable experience, and he really pushed me to my limits, but I learned all about composition, understood the importance of details, and worked hard and delivered quality work. I had a love/hate relationship with him, but nothing but massive amounts of respect for the man.

Christian Nordland is another memorable colleague; I first had the pleasure of hiring him at my own agency and then later joined him at another agency. He's a highly creative person I respect and enjoyed working with. Bernt Dag Ravnevand was a very good friend and CEO, but he also reignited my interest for Liverpool FC back in the days. Finn Roger was a perfectionist when it comes to image reproduction and retouch. Thanks to Kjell-Ove, Heidi, and so many more amazing creatives from my time in the south of Norway.

If I were to write all the names of all the people who have inspired me and influenced me in some shape or form, this book would be twice as long, and though I do want to give credit where credit is due, I will limit this to people who changed my life for the better:

Marius Eriksen invited me to an interview based on a tweet I sent him, asking for a job. We met, and one hour later, I was hired as the creative director and social media strategist at Norway's first and best social media agency. I thank him for taking the chance and giving me the base to progress and grow.

Nina O'Gorman was a firm but inspirational leader at Creuna, where I served as creative director and worked with some amazing people and teams; Marthe & Martine, Pål & Ove, Jonas and Jahn Tore, Alexander, Birgitte, Severin, Trine, Hilde, and so many more talented people at that agency, way too many to mention.

Then my time at DDB, which was initiated by Hans Petter Stub, Pelle Josephson, and Niclas Melin, taking me in as their chief innovation officer and for working on some great brands and projects, pushing the boundaries and inspiring clients for change.

Now it's time for honourable mentions from the amazing Ogilvy group, first point of contact being Rohit Bhargava, who introduced me to Nando Rodriguez (Global HR) and connected me to Gemma Craven, Marshall Manson, Leo Ryan, Thomas Crayton, Laura Brown, Laurie Close, and James Whatley. Amazingly inspiring people I loved working with and getting to know, and some even becoming good friends as well.

Here comes a long list of people I have had the pleasure of meeting and I have been so fortunate and happy to have in my network, as speakers to some of my events, and some as close friends: Rohit Bhargava, David Rosenberg, Guy Kawasaki, Chris Anderson (TED), Mitch Joel, David Armano, Thomas Marzano, Shane Steele, Adam Ostrow, Kyle Lacy,

Ryan Bonnici, Derek Laney, Maggie Fox, Jacob Morgan, Chris Brogan, Tara Hunt, Lars Silberbauer, Viveka von Rosen, Lauren Rubin, Callan Green, Ric Dragon, Jon Lombardo, Scott Monty, Rob Newlan, Lisa Hu, Babba Canales, Peter Zakharov, Jonathan Forrester, David Rock (drock), Eric Fulwiler, Seth Godin, and Gary Vaynerchuk.

I saw Vaynerchuk on stage in London back in 2008, and I just went up and asked him after if he would join me and Thomas Moen (see next person) on our podcast show, *Sofaprat* (Couchtalk), and it initiated a friendship that has lasted up until this day, because of that first meeting. He is cut-throat clear on his opinions, no filter, and he is honest to the bone. He has been a speaker at my conference and has been on my podcast; we've had dinners and drinks with solid inspirational conversations, and I love the dude. He is a hustler and an attention-trader by far.

Thomas Moen is a near and dear friend of mine who challenged and supported me through some rough times and good times; he was the cohost of Sofaprat, our first video-podcast-show we started back in 2009. His talent for knowing what to focus on, for prioritizing, for setting realistic goals, and for making shit happen is truly inspirational and impressive. He has a heart of gold and just makes everyone feel good by his presence, and our friendship is one of those that you know will last a lifetime.

James Towers, my Australian legend friend, always gives a smile and support, regardless of topic and time. He's a brilliant marketing hustler and a solid friend who is always there with positivity and a strong mindset. He has a view of life which I admire: to enjoy it, focus on the right things, and hackle through difficulties, and even though he is limited for time, he is always there to have your back if you ask for it. He's a brilliant plodder and someone I respect, admire, and love.

Chris Lawrence is from New York and another of my very closest friends. We connected in the lunchroom at a coworking space over a mutual passion of ours, Ducati, which then grew into a friendship. We have worked together, travelled together, climbed the tallest Nordic mountain together, spent a month in Italy (best summer ever), and have a common strength in communication, which brings deep conversations and support for one another when needed. He also helped me nail the title of this book, so thank you for that, Chris. He's got the moves on the dance floor like no other, he is light and fun to hang around with, but he's also a solid friend and sounding board when I feel a bit lost, discouraged, or out of form. Love to you, buddy.

James Whatley is my creative counterpart in the UK; currently with Digitas, James is brilliant and an overall nerd in all things digital, which I love, but also a person I admire and get so much positive energy from whenever we hang out together or talk. I've been told that I am a curious person, but I feel I can say with confidence that James surpasses me massively in that department. We can be vulnerable together, and even though we don't see each other often, we know we have a solid friendship for a lifetime. Cheers and love to you, mate.

Simon Sanebak is my attention wizard, an overall energetic dude who has been a strong support over the past years. We met at a conference we both spoke at back in 2013, and from there, we stayed in touch, before getting closer as both friends, mentors, and colleagues. What impresses me with Simon is his loyalty, his kindness, and his supportiveness. I have nothing but gratitude for his friendship and presence in my life. Love.

Maani Safa is my brother from another mother, which is the best definition of our relationship. I met Maani at SxSW back in 2013 and was impressed with his presentation on stage. We connected, I visited him in London a few times, and we have stayed in touch over these years. Our friendship has grown with common interests and passions but mostly the values and principles we live by. We are completely different but, at the same time, so similar in the way we think, perform, and work; it is an absolute energy boost whenever we talk, because it just clicks and fits. Massive respect and love to you, my dapper friend.

I probably forgot to mention several people, and I left some out because they didn't have a direct impact to me in context to this book, but they shouldn't be insulted by this. I know their importance, but it's more a consideration to the readers of this book and the connection to the message. I am only an email click away, so feel free to reach out anytime.

As I mentioned in the start of this book, I dedicate this book to my parents and my kids. Natalie is my precious, and she has always been my precious since I came into her life in 1993, when she was four years old. She has grown into a woman, a mother, and a doctor. To say that I am proud of her is an understatement. She has been such a spark in my life, and I vividly remember the day at the age of five when she asked if it was okay to call me "Dad." Ah, my heart melted right there and then. Love beyond words.

Kris Isak is my oldest son. It was such a proud and amazing sensation to watch this skinny, dark-haired kid grow into the man he is today. We worked together, we sweated at the gym together, and I had the pleasure of seeing him excel and become independent and successful on his own. His charm, his energy, his drive, and his skills in closing sales are unmatched, except by his younger brother, who executes them in different ways. I love you.

This leads us to my youngest son, Arnt David, who impresses me every single day. His ability to adapt and consume information, connect the dots, read people, and understand their needs and challenges, and even better, overcome them, has left me speechless more than once. Arnt David is the next generation of successful entrepreneurs; he brings devotion, dedication, passion, drive, and enthusiasm to make things happen. He is agile and adaptive but also compassionate; he has so many qualities that I admire and love more than a dad, but also as a person. Love you, more.

It is safe to say, I am blessed to have these three wonderful and amazing humans in my life, and I have nothing but gratitude that they are in my life. They are my motivation, my strength, and the reason I challenge myself to make today better than yesterday.

I am also connected to many amazing people who have made an impact on my life in different ways. One thing I can safely say is, yes, everything happens for a reason, and I am thankful and filled with joy for everyone who has affected me in one way, shape, or form, beautifully explained in this quote, which is also the conclusion to this book:

Never blame anyone in life.

The good people give you happiness.

The worst people give you a lesson.

And the best people ...

give you memories.

Arnt

Lightning Source UK Ltd.
Milton Keynes UK
UKHW041441221021
392664UK00001B/136